EquiChord's Rhythm Riding
A Guide to Riding with Music

CeCe and Frank Maddlone
In Collaboration and Consultation with:
Dr. Cesar Parra

MarMadd Publishing

Published by MarMadd Publishing

Printed in the United States of America

Book and Graphic Designs by EquiChord
© 2008 EquiChord

Library of Congress Certificate Number Pending

ISBN13 978-0-9670900-1-6

Contents

Acknowledgement

Whenever a journey begins, one hopes to encounter the paths of least resistance. We have been very fortunate to be guided by truly inspirational beacons who helped make the voyage to our destination an enlightening and rewarding experience. Our first and brightest light has been Rebecca Langwost-Barlow. Her support and to-the-point advice was always available to us. Without her initial encouragement, this project would have been easily detoured. The next shimmering light that beckoned us forward was Rebecca Didier from Trafalgar. Along with Martha Cook, Rebecca beguiled us into developing a project that called upon us to document the best we had to offer from our knowledge and life's experiences.

Of the many equestrian luminaries we have had the pleasure to encounter, none have been more gracious than Dr. Cesar Parra. Without his insightful and brilliant perspectives and the incredible education we've received from him, we would not have taken the steps to expand the book to encompass the larger frontiers. His knowledge and generosity are boundless, and we are honored to know him, work with him, and count him as a friend.

We would like to express our extreme gratitude to both Dr. Volker Moritz and Nicole Uphoff-Selke for granting us so much of their valuable time, knowledge, and insights. Their wonderfully magnetic personalities are only exceeded by their incredible talents as educators and dressage evangelists.

Finally, we would like to thank those miraculous connectors who have made all the difference in our world. To Barbara Strawson, for her thoughtful support, and to the Ladies of Wyndham Oaks for continuing to dance with such joy. To Marco Marinangeli & Simone Sello - truly the best musicians and friends anyone could possibly claim. A very special hug goes out to Maria Potter - without her unselfish help and support, we would have vanished quietly into the night. To Mike Liddell, master wordsmith, educator, and writer extraordinaire, for his gracious support and firm editorial hand. These folks are stalwart examples of humanity at its best, and we are honored to be a part of their lives. This is dedicated to our parents for always being with us, and to our dearest friends, who never stopped believing in us.

1

Foreword

Our Story

Our official Freestyle journey began on a late summer's day at a recognized horse show in Middleburg, VA. My wife, a lover of all things equestrian and particularly dressage, had been trying to entice me into the world of musical Freestyles. As a music educator, producer, and lyricist, as well as a re-specter of horses at a distance - a great distance - I was none too keen at the prospect. However, I wanted to see what the fuss was all about, as well as help my wife's dream of danc-ing with her horse become a reality. As I watched my first Freestyle, I exclaimed in awe, "the horse is dancing with the music!", and then added, "the music is horrible!" My wife looked at me and smiled with that "I told you so" look. From that point on, I was hooked and EquiChord was born. Since its inception, our goal has been the promotion and elevation of the Kür by raising the bar on the musical, tech-nological, and performance aspects of the sport.

Frank Maddlone

Mr. Maddlone is truly one of the rare renaissance men. He began his formal musical studies in 1970 at the Conservatory of Music in Puerto Rico under the tutelage of such artistic luminaries as Angeles Otein, Sergie Rainis, and Pablo Casals. Although his primary studies were as a classically trained singer, Frank opted for a degree in music education, receiv-ing his B.A. in 1975. After moving to Los Angeles in 1979 where he worked as a bilingual elementary education teacher, Frank began to pursue his interests in technology, receiving a certification in computer programming and design in 1984. That same year, Frank partnered with the award-winning composer & producer Marco Marinangeli and formed MarMadd Music, a studio that was at the forefront of musical computer composition and engineering. With their unique combination of live instrumentation and cutting edge technology, they worked in the music industry on a variety of film and television projects, as well as with several solo artists both in the U.S. and abroad. In 1987, they were the recipients of the OTI Music Award in Los Angeles. In 1993, Frank established TechnaChord as an independent technology consultancy firm reporting on the emerging portable technology markets. His writings have been showcased on FoxPop.com and CNN, and was a guest speaker at such venues as the CTIA, DCI, Field Force Automation, MobileVillage's Technology Expo, and PC Expo. Since its inception, TechnaChord has evolved into a collaborative creative trust with alliance partners located throughout the United States. Its purpose is to merge the availability and innovation of technology with the creative aspects of musical and multimedia production. Some of TechnaChord's more recent collaborative projects include an educational children's music CD for Fisher-Price, and a practice CD with all original music designed as part of EquiChord's Rhythm Riding Training Series.

For the past several years, Frank has been working on a series of books whose subjects range from ethics in technology to education. His passion for music and computers collided with his wife's passion for dance and horses, and he has since been collaborating in the development of new and innovative musical projects for the equestrian community in the area of dressage freestyle. Frank has been an active member of ASCAP *(American Society of Composers, Authors and Publishers)* for over 23 years, as well as a member of SIAE *(Societa Italiana degli Autori ed Editori)*. He has also held the office of chapter president for the MENC *(Music Educators National Conference)*.

CeCe Maddlone

Ms. Maddlone's love affair with performance and horses began at the tender age of three, when she began her formal training in art, dance, riding, and music. As a member of a family filled with professional musicians, opera singers, artists and educators, the performance arts became second nature to her. Her formative years were spent studying piano, ballet, and choreography with instructors from the Royal Ballet, American Ballet Theater, Martha Graham, David Howard, Melissa Hayden, and Merce Cunningham, to name but a few. At 12, she began performing, demonstrating, and teaching as part of her dance apprenticeship with the Minnesota Dance Theatre. Her formal education naturally progressed to Theater Arts, where she was nominated for the Irene Ryan Award and placed number one in her region during the URTA *(University Resident Theater Association)* competitions. Although she was offered several university fellowships to teach and continue on with her graduate studies in Theater Arts and Dance, Ms. Maddlone decided to continue performing and teaching in the private sector for over eighteen years, ultimately moving into the business world as a Corporate Trainer and Director of Marketing. She has choreographed for professional and amateur productions alike, as well as directed and staged numerous fashion shows and TV commercials. Ms. Maddlone is currently producing the original Rhythm Riding Series for EquiChord, as well as collaborating on several articles, books, and DVDs. Her ongoing passion for horses and Dressage has always played an integral part in her experiences. Dancing on horseback and creating dances with horses is the natural evolution of a lifetime.

EquiChord

EquiChord is a professional music studio based on the United States' East Coast. They are honored and pleased to be providing their works to talented riders of all levels. Through seamless musical arrangements, choreography, and original compositions that touch all genres, EquiChord combines state of the art technologies with a high degree of artistry to each Freestyle. EquiChord is available for seminars, clinics, and individual sessions. Recently, their musical freestyle seminar/clinic was approved for USDF University Credit.

For more information, please visit:

http://www.EquiChord.com

Introduction

A Brief History

*"Music is a universal art - it speaks to each being
through the rhythm in their heart"*
Franco Ponti

"Dressage" is the French word for training. Generally, it is often thought of as that stuffy, boring sport where riders in top hats sit on their horses and look pretty - or, as some horse husbands might comment, "is as much fun as watching paint dry". After all, it doesn't involve careening cross-country over jumps or leaping giant obstacles in a single bound. However, the basics of dressage are the basics of all good riding. Mastering these over time can sculpt a horse into a work of art with the agility, strength, and grace to elevate even the most mundane movement into a dance.

Over the last few of decades, another dimension has been introduced to the sport that has rekindled a growing excitement in its audience - the Musical Freestyle or **Kür**. The musical portions of most competitions are actually selling out and even drawing in non-dressage enthusiasts. Why? Because there is nothing more breathtaking than to watch these magnificent creatures and their talented riders perform to all genres of music. In the last decade, it has become the fastest growing segment of the sport!

Adding the musical Freestyle as a component to the recognized Dressage competition did not come easy. Many felt that it would degrade the sport and reduce it to the level of a circus performance. Some still hold on to these views, reticent to allow for the natural evolution of the artistic elements. However, defining a spectacular dressage routine as "art" or a "performance" cannot lessen its impact; it merely broadens the standards for all to enjoy and appreciate.

Webster Defines *Art* as:
"The expression or application of human creative skill and imagination - a skill at doing a specified thing, typically one acquired through practice."

Webster Defines *Performance* as:
"The action or process of carrying out or accomplishing an action, task, or function."

A well-executed and scored musical Freestyle is truly the application of human creative skill and imagination acquired through practice and carried out to fruition, thus becoming performance art. In essence, it is the perfect union of art and technique.

Introductory Exercise:
Step One
Acclimating Your Horse to Music

Introducing Music

 The one thing that can stop a good Freestyle in its tracks is a horse that is frightened by the music or speakers. We have been pleasantly surprised at how quickly most horses respond positively to music if they have been properly introduced to the concept of recorded sound. When horses respond unfavorably, it is usually because they have undergone a bad experience. Introduce your horse to the music in a slow, quiet, nonchalant manner. Make sure your sound system does not crackle, sputter, or produce loud feedback. There are "hot spots" on every stage or arena where the speakers cross and the music is louder. Start with the volume low and hand walk your horse first through the "hot spots" - directly under the speakers - so that the increased volume doesn't startle them. As your sessions continue, gradually increase the volume. Make sure your first sessions are fun and relaxing, with the sole purpose and focus being on the music.

7

PRINCIPLES OF DRESSAGE

The object of dressage is the gradual development of the horse and rider into happy and harmonious athletes. This goal is achieved through a process of consistent and conscientious training that will ultimately result in a horse that is calm, supple, loose, and flexible. From this basis, a confident and attentive horse can truly become a keen partner.

These qualities are revealed by:

- ☐ Rhythm and Relaxation
- ☐ Lightness and Ease of movement
- ☐ Willingness to move forward from the hind quarters and lightly off the forehand in a straight and balanced fashion
- ☐ The Acceptance and Connection of the bridle

The horse learns to respond to the lightest of aids and develops the coordination and musculature to achieve true self-carriage. Therefore, all the movements required of the horse should be performed in a calm, balanced fashion with the appropriate straightness on a straight line and bend on a curved line. Although the terms "calm" and "relaxed" are frequently used, this does not mean that a horse can be sluggish or inactive. The horse must be constantly active and energetic without any tension or resistance. The fluidity of the movements should be expressed by the suppleness of the joints and the consistency of the gaits. In all the work, even at the halt, the horse must be "on the bit". A horse is said to be "on the bit" when they are actively moving from behind over the top of a relaxed back through a curved, flexible neck that is reaching gently into the bit, and back around almost in a complete circular fashion. Regardless of the transition between or within each gait, the head should remain in a steady position. As a rule, it should be slightly in front of the vertical, with a supple poll as the highest point of the neck.

Rhythm is fundamental to dressage.

Preface
How To Use This Book

"The earth has music for those who listen."
Shakespeare

This book is structured very much like the various dressage levels. Each chapter builds on the previous one, thus enabling the reader to develop a better understanding of riding with music, rhythm, choreography, and its related requirements. The starting point is, as always, the de-facto rules as set forth by the **FEI** *(Federation Equestre Internationale)* and the various organizations around the world. From there, the book expands into the practical functional aspects relating to Freestyles. This book was inspired from the myriad questions both amateur and professional riders alike have posed over the years regarding everything from beats to rules. In an effort to demystify the Freestyle process, we decided to put together a clear, central resource and reference guide that addresses the practical mechanics of creating a Freestyle.

This book is divided into two segments - the lower and the upper levels. It is a valuable step-by-step resource for those venturing into the art of the Kür for the first time, and for those who are already in the process, regardless of their level. Those who are actively coaching, teaching, or training will find this to be an invaluable addition to their teaching curriculum. Each chapter starts with the foundation of technique, explores the addition of music, and culminates with reinforcing exercises. The reader can immediately apply those new elements while riding with the accompanying **Rhythm Riding Practice CD**. This combination provides an opportunity to take the knowledge garnered from this book and interactively apply it in the arena.

The companion CD contains over 60 minutes of original music designed specifically for horses and their riders. It is divided into two parts: The first is a 22-minute warm-up with varying tempos between walk, trot, and canter, allowing the rider to work on transitions without worrying about changing music. The second portion contains the practice music formatted into a 5-minute Freestyle. Within the CD you may choose the track that best approximates your horse's BPMs - Large Pony/Small Horse, Medium Horse, or Large Horse.

Although this book utilizes an amalgam of rules and regulations gathered from the various associations around the world as its foundation, they are merely solid training reference points through which everyone may benefit. The earlier a horse and rider's training can develop the skill-sets required to ride with music, the more holistic and creative their performance will be. This is also a great resource for instructors, trainers, and anyone who is working with music. In order to assure consistency and accuracy in your performance, please be sure to consult your region's association or governing board for rules specific to Freestyles.

her of the Lundquist Dressage Scholarship, Becky trained in Germany with the late Reiner Klimke. She has always been committed to competing her own FEI and young horses as well as bringing along her own students and client horses. As an active instructor, clinician, and seasoned competitor, Becky has the distinction of being the only rider in her region to win the finals on the same horse at both Prix St. George and Intermediare-1 in the same year. She is a USDF Gold Medalist and USDF certified instructor through fourth level.

Becky is a strong advocate of the Kür. Along with actively performing her own Freestyles, she has brilliantly choreographed pieces for her students of all levels. It is rare to find such an accomplished rider who also has an innate sense for music and movement. Becky has created choreography for winning Quadrilles, Pas de Deux, and exhibition rides.

EquiChord is proud to provide Becky and her students with Freestyle music of all genres.

An Interview with Rebecca Langwost-Barlow

When you approach a freestyle, do you first start with the choreography or the music?

I've done it both ways. In my case, I tend to listen to different pieces of music and pick out the ones that I like. I've always been a theme person, so I like to choose music *(and a freestyle)* that has a theme - I can't stand listening to music from different places and having it put together in a disjointed way, it makes me crazy. When choosing a theme, it doesn't matter whether it comes from a musical motif, a particular artist, or a particular type of music. So, I always start with that, riding to each piece of music to see which parts fit the horse or the movements that are required in the freestyle. I then string the pieces together accordingly, and send them along to my favorite musicians and ask them if can we put it together this way or that. I don't do all the choreography and then add the music, and I don't do the music and then add all the choreography - I do a little of both. The choreography evolves out of the different verses of the music. Now when it comes to a quadrille, the situation is a little bit different. I have to get four horses with different rhythms, four different types of riders and put it all together accordingly. What I end up doing is making the choreography as dramatic as possible, and then having the musicians put the music together in a way that will make the movements even more dynamic than it looks.

What do you see as the biggest stumbling blocks for freestyles right now in terms of participation?

OK, this is one of my biggest issues. I think that, in order to make freestyles more interesting and popular, there needs to be more showmanship thrown into the mix - especially with the younger folks coming into the sport. There are few adults out there that have a better imagination than a child. In order to make it fun and keep the interest going, horses and riders should be allowed to wear certain types of cos-

13

tumes during their performances. Additionally, they should create fun costume classes for kids - they would be more apt to participate if creativity were part of the scoring, not just trying to put the horse on the bit. Kids are really motivated to do a good job, and a costumed division would make it so much more interesting. Adults can do this but on a different level - if you want to bring fresh blood into the sport, you have to open it up to that kind of a format. Allow for just a little bit more showmanship - that's the best way to describe it. I know that a lot of people are afraid to make it look a little too "circus", but you have to be realistic about this if you want young kids - especially those that don't have particularly fancy horses - to find a way to compete, and this would be a good way to go about doing it.

What is your definition of a "circus" performance?

Well, I won't use that as my own definition, but I can tell you how people view it. Some people disregard the quality of the ride and the dressage aspect of it to do something fancy and flamboyant, and forget that this is basically a dressage test where the horse has to be ridden well and correctly, and not move up the ladder because the horse is able to do one trick particularly well and not much of anything else. And basically that's what people see as the "circus"; it becomes more of a show than a good dressage test. But I still feel there's got to be a middle ground.

What do you think of as the ultimate performance freestyle? What aspects of the freestyle make it a memorable performance versus a routine with background music?

For me, the performance that is memorable is one that plays on the drama of the music, fitting it seamlessly with the horse and the way it's ridden. My all-time favorite ride 'til this day is Anky (*Anky van Grunsven*) on Bonfire. I know that she has gotten higher scores on other horses, and that there are other great tests out there. But when I see her doing her old test on Bonfire, I still get a little chill; it's just great. She does a perfect build up at the onset of the routine,

14

then brings in an element of rest to soften the mood. It's like classical music - it builds you up a little, then calms you down, then gets you excited again, only to calm you down once again - that, to me, is a great freestyle.

Why do you think Anky has been able to stay at the level where she's at, maintaining that place even though she may not necessarily have the best horses?

She obviously has an incredible musical ear, which a lot of riders don't have *(which I find kind of funny, because we ride to rhythm)*. There are a lot of people that unfortunately have a tin ear, and cannot hear the subtle changes needed in the performance. Anky obviously has a great ear, and can even sing which we heard in her last freestyle. She knows exactly when to pump her horse up in time with the music, and that's key to a great routine. That's what makes her a cut above everyone else, no matter who they may be.

So you classify her as being able to do the ultimate, of having technique, of combining great music and creating a good performance in the realm of dressage.

As far as I'm concerned, there's no one that comes close to her. It's my own opinion; I've seen many freestyles, and seen many that I love to watch, but I never get disappointed watching Anky. She knows how to make a horse look the part, and appear as though he's listening to the music as well. I love to watch her ride.

Do you ever think that freestyles in the lower levels will become mandatory?

I do, actually. I believe that they will become mandatory, because the associations want to keep finding new ways of encouraging people into the sport, and this event *(freestyles)* have a great appeal with the public. It's funny that in the US, freestyles have proven to be a good thing because there are so many different levels of riders and horses that it does level out the playing field to a certain extent. In Europe, they don't do the lower level freestyles - it's for FEI horses, unless that has changed recently, which I don't think it has. They feel that it could be something that is detrimental to horses moving up the ladder. But a lot of horses can only get to a certain level and need a place to go, and freestyles could provide them with that avenue. So, yes - I do think that they're going to become mandatory - it may not be necessary, but would really be a good avenue to pursue.

What benefits you think riders can get from riding with music or riding freestyles when they're starting out?

The main thing, for me, is that it teaches them to relax, to focus on the rhythm of the horse - it keeps you riding at a certain tempo, and helps to make you sharper. I think it also makes you a better rider because the music keeps you honest; it's constantly telling you where you should be, what the movement should be, what the timing should be, what the tempo should be, thus making you a more rounded, more aware rider. I've seen a bunch of people who do a great job riding quadrilles - they don't ride their tests so well, but they ride those quadrilles fantastic because they have to keep up with the most powerful or the most forward horse. It pushes them a little bit beyond their limits, and makes them a better rider. It's like when I play tennis, I play a lot better when I play with a more advanced opponent than when I play with a beginner.

What do you think the element of musical freestyles has brought to the sport of dressage?

At first I wasn't totally sold on it, because I felt that it would have been better if kids were doing it. Like I said earlier, I don't want to make it sound like a circus, but I saw it more as a costumed event, with kids being the main protagonists because they can be so much fun. But when I went to Las Vegas and realized just how huge this kind of event could be, I saw how great its potential could be for the sport across

16

the board. It could be enormous if showcased a couple of times around the country with really good FEI freestyles as the main attraction. I mean, the lower level stuff is a little hard to watch sometimes, especially if the music is not chosen very well or the horse is not very good, or the dressage is not very good. Let's face it; if the music is fantastic but the dressage is ugly, then it's not a very good show to watch. In that regard, we have a long way to go. I think that there could be tremendous possibilities for improvement if there were ways to encourage more riders - like establishing a couple of prize money freestyles, that's a good start. A lot of it is really intimidating because of the expense - a lot of these choreographed routines cost thousands of dollars, and few people have that kind of money to spend. Especially if you're doing this only for one horse, and the horse moves up a level or breaks down - it doesn't necessarily mean that the next one is going to work with that same music. I think that there are a lot of aspects that have to be worked out, but the potential is certainly there.

What do you think the future will be for freestyles?

Well, I think it's gotten very sophisticated, and it is only going to become even more so down the line. People now have access to editing technology, better horses, and better riders. I think that when you add music and choreography - your own choreography, the sky's the limit. With those elements in play, I think it's only going to get better.

Chapter One

The ABCs

"A horse, a horse! My kingdom for a horse!"
Shakespeare

Let's imagine that the arena is a stage or, better yet, a blank canvas. Entering onto the freshly smoothed footing, your horse's hooves draw their patterns upon its blank surface. As you leave the arena and look back, you see the finished portrait of what you and your horse have created. Whenever you ride, you are preparing to perform a series of movements or patterns whether by design, instruction, or improvisation. In essence, you are choreographing. Yes, you are! Like all languages, there is a basic set of symbols that are learned to create words. In order to consistently repeat a particular series of well-executed patterns in riding or choreography, certain points of reference or symbols are necessary.

Having a set of visible signposts allows any rider to consistently hit their mark when repeating a sequence of movements or re-creating choreography. The dressage letters and their sequence are universally accepted markers for everyone to follow. By incorporating them into a system of notation that can represent a series of movements, complex patterns, tests and designs, completed routines can then be accurately written down for future reference and as a tangible way to create Freestyle choreography.

18

Where Did They Come From?

Inevitably someone will ask, "Where did the arena letters come from?" When equestrian events were added to the 1912 Olympics, there was no sign of the letters. Eight years later, they made their first appearance at the 1920 games. Although no one is precisely sure where the letters and their order originated, there are a several conjectures. One of the most popular theories explains that the letters were borrowed from the old Imperial German Palace Stables. Around the large courtyard, there were markers posted every few feet to indicate where the grooms stood at the ready, holding their assigned mounts for members of the imperial court and their guests. Since the yards were large enough to double as schooling arenas, the markers probably served as convenient reference points as well.

Here is what the markers may have originally stood for:

K	Kaiser/Konig	= Emperor/King
F	Furst	= Prince
V	Vassal	= Servant/squire/equerry
P	Pferdknecht/Ostler	= Groom
E	Edeling/Ehrengast	= Guest of honor
B	Bannertrager	= Standard Bearer
S	Schatzkanzler	= Chancellor of the Exchequer
R	Ritter	= Knight
H	Hofmarschall	= Lord Chancellor
M	Meier *(Meister)*	= Steward
A	Ausgang	= Exit

What Are They For?

It is often said that timing is everything, and intimately knowing your arena facilitates the musical and choreographic process. What do we mean by that? Riding times are of the utmost importance, especially when riding with music. Time will lead to tempo, which will lead to rhythm - but that's a story for a later chapter. When beginning to develop a Freestyle, start by understanding your individual times. This is one of many instances when knowing the arena and its letters will be extremely handy. The best way to tackle the whole is by starting with the small pieces. Learn the basic perimeter letters first:

A K E H C M B F
(All King Edward's Horses Can Manage Big Fences)

Always remember that **X** is the center of the arena.

Definition:
Arena |ə ˈrēnə| |ə ˌrinə| |ə ˌriːnə|
Noun
A level area surrounded by seats for spectators in which sports, entertainments, and other public events are held.

ORIGIN early 17th cent.: from Latin *harena*, arena 'sand, sand-strewn place of combat.'

Requirements for Dressage Competition The Arena

Dimensions:

Small Arena: 20 x 40 meters
(approx. 66' x 132')

Standard Arena: 20 x 60 meters
(approx. 66' x 198')*

*All FEI and most non-FEI tests are performed in a standard sized arena, including musical Freestyles. Therefore, we are using the standard arena measurements for choreography, distances, and times.

Step One in the Process:
Know Your Arena and Your Times

Many of you probably already know the arena letters, but bear with me, there is more. After you have learned your letters, start measuring your times and counts. The easiest way to measure is by knowing how long it takes to ride from letter to letter in each gait, and how many counts that translates into. For example, how long it takes to perform a 20m circle at the working trot to the right at **E**, or how long it takes to do a free walk across the diagonal from **H** to **F** (*see exercises at the end of the chapter*). The letters are our primer for building a Freestyle, just as the alphabet is our primer for building words, phrases, sentences, paragraphs, and completed thoughts, or as musical notes are to creating a song.

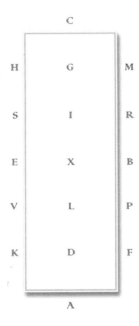

Step Two in the Process:
Know Your Arena and Your Times

Recommended Exercise

 If your arena doesn't already have letters, purchase or make a set by printing out each letter in a large, bolded font on card stock paper and have them laminated. They are extremely helpful, regardless of what type of riding you do!

Ride these basic figures and time them *(it is best if you can have someone videotape these. You can also use the same videotape to figure out your BPMs)*:

1. 20-meter circle at the free walk, working trot and canter to the right and left
2. Crossing the long diagonal through **X** at the free walk, working trot, and canter
3. Traveling down the long side at the free walk, working trot, and canter
4. Traveling down the short side at the free walk, working trot, and canter
5. Three loop serpentine from **A** to **C** at the working trot using full width of the arena
6. Four loop serpentine from **A** to **C** at the working trot from quarter-line to quarter-line

Practice the precision of these exercises with the letters and start riding the patterns along with the **Rhythm Riding Practice CD.**

Draw out a standard size arena with the letters, and then draw out the figures you have just timed and record your times. As you progress in your training, retake your times and see how they have changed.

Lower and Upper Levels

In order to appreciate the schooling progression of a dressage horse, it is necessary to first understand how the education of the horse and rider is developed around the world. Essentially, both are expected to pass a series of tests before they can advance onto the next level. Within each, there are a number of skill-sets that have to be achieved before passing from test to test, and from level to level. Each country has their own way of dividing up these lower level tests. For example, in the United States and Canada, a rider must progress through four "Levels" before graduating to an international level of competition. In England, the progression follows from Novice, Elementary, Medium, Advanced Medium, to Advanced and, in the rest of Europe, it's delineated as Basic, Intermediate, and Advance. Recently, the American governing body *(USEF)* proposed putting a new Performance Standards into effect that would more closely resemble the European model.

Once a competing team has passed through the lower levels, they become eligible to compete at **FEI**. **FEI**, or **Federation Equestre Internationale**, is the international governing body for all Olympic equestrian disciplines.

At international competitions regulated by the **FEI**, riders and horses are expected to perform the following tests:

- Prix St. Georges *(of medium standard)*
- Intermediare 1 *(advanced standard)*
- Intermediare 2 *(advanced standard)*
- Grand Prix
- Grand Prix Special
- Grand Prix Freestyle *(**Kür**)* or the musical Freestyle

Although Freestyles are not yet universally required at lower levels of competition, they are gaining wide popularity and appeal from riders and spectators alike. It has been the view of many high level trainers and educators that Freestyles should not be performed at the lower levels, since they feel that technique is often sacrificed for the fun of riding with music. However, many instructors who have incorporated music into their training, schooling, and instruction have found it extremely beneficial in teaching the fundamentals of rhythm and relaxation. Since the artistic aspects of a well-performed Freestyle cannot be accomplished without a certain degree of technical proficiency as a foundation, many instructors are finding that adding the Freestyle component to a rider's earlier education can inspire a higher degree of technical accomplishment.

Riding Skills Required For Each Level

Finding the right movements and weaving them into an appealing pattern is one of the most creative aspects of developing a good Freestyle design - especially at the lower levels. Since a rider is penalized heavily for executing elements above their level, it is extremely important to know and understand what movements are acceptable and go from there. Fortunately, there are very precise guidelines and requirements laid out for each level by the governing bodies within each country or region. Although there is no official universal standard that defines level progression before a competitor reaches FEI, the basic goals and requirements are roughly the same. In accordance with the standards set forth by these governing bodies, we have compiled "cheat sheets" that will aid you in putting together fun, choreographic patterns while staying within the prescribed boundaries. We recommend that you refer to the page that has your level while you are drawing out your patterns, so that you may precisely gauge your level of movements. Be sure to refer to the governing body within your own country and region to ensure you have the exact requirements for competition.

For a complete list of associations around the world, please refer to *Appendix 6*. Below is a brief list of a few of the international organizations:

The British Dressage Association *(BDF)*

British Dressage was set up in 1998 to govern the sport under the **British Equestrian Federation** *(BEF)*. **BDF** has established their own set of pre-**FEI** qualifications. They are also responsible for the development of their own Freestyle Tests and rules.

The Canadian Dressage Owners & Riders Association

(CADORA)

CADORA was established in 1969 as a national non-profit organization dedicated to the education and advancement of dressage in Canada. As an affiliate member of **Equine Canada**, **CADORA's** goal has been to develop their riders in a manner that is consistent with the principles of Dressage as formulated by the international governing body of equestrian Olympic disciplines, the **FEI**.

Dressage Canada *(DC)*

Like **CADORA, Dressage Canada's** objective is to foster the growth of Dressage at the local, national, and international levels. **DC** provides support and guidance to both amateur and professionals through the following programs: Coaching education and programs, officials education and programs, rules & qualifying criteria, sport development, publications, and awards. **DC** is a discipline sub-committee under **Equine Canada**, the **National Equestrian Federation of Canada**.

French Equestrian Federation *(FFE)*

In 1921, the **Fédération Française des Sports Equestres** was formed to govern over all things equestrian in France. The **FFE** is a member of the **Federation Equestre Internationale** *(FEI)* and the **National Olympic Committee and Sports French (CNOSF)**

The German National Equestrian Federation *(FN)*

The umbrella organization for all aspects of horsemanship, breeding, training, and education in Germany. The **FN** is also responsible for the promotion of upper-level competitions and is affiliated with both the **German Equestrian Olympics Committee** *(DOKR)* and the **Federal Service Center** *(BIC)*. In 1998, the **German Academy of the Horse** was formed to provide advanced education to professionals and non-professionals alike.

The United States Dressage Federation *(USDF)*

The **USDF** was established in 1973 with the express purpose of educating and promoting dressage, as well as to recognize achievement. Through the **USDF**, we have seen the development of their University and a variety of curricula dedicated to the advancement of the sport. The **USDF** creates the lower level Freestyle and Pas De Deux standards as well as the compulsory Quadrille tests.

The United States Equestrian Federation *(USEF)*

The **USEF** was established in 1917 to create competitive uniformity at equestrian competitions. Over the years, it has maintained its primary purpose as well as developed rule books that not only deal with aspects of competition, but also fairness and equine welfare. For dressage, the **USEF** develops the compulsory tests for Training through Fourth Level. However, the **USDF** develops the lower level Freestyle and Pas De Deux standards, as well as the compulsory Quadrille tests.

Eligibility for Competition

The Dressage Musical Freestyle portion of the competition is meant to showcase the abilities of the rider within their own level of competition. As it is often said in the dance world, technique is the foundation of all great art. Therefore, the technical portion of the ride has equal weight to the artistic. To ensure that riders can demonstrate required proficiency,

26

they are encouraged to compete at their level or, preferably, at one level below where they are schooling. In most areas, in order to even enter a Freestyle class, a horse/rider combination has to have received a basic score requirement or number of points. For example, the **USDF** currently requires *a score of 58% in the highest test of the declared freestyle level.*[1]

58% - What Does That Mean?

Each level has a number of tests. Each test advances in skill, with the last test in the sequence being the most difficult. For example, the **USEF** currently designates that First Level Test 4 is the most advanced within that level. In order for riders to compete in a First Level Freestyle, they must have received a score of at least 58% on the First Level Test 4 compulsory test. Commonly, riders will do a Freestyle at one level below where they are competing technically. Therefore, if a rider is competing at Second Level in the **USEF** current system, then they would be eligible to compete in a First Level Freestyle class.

Reading a Compulsory Test

First off, let's explain the difference between a compulsory and a Freestyle test. The compulsory routines are designed to test the rider's ability to perform required sequences of movements according to acceptable standards. These are the tests that are published by the governing bodies of each association within each country. This chapter of the book provides the basic Freestyle requirements and technical elements for the various levels. In our attempt to assemble a universal guide to outline the requirements and elements for each level, our charts demonstrate a compilation and comparison drawn from several of the international associations. Once again, it is important that you consult the Rules and Regulations within your own country and region. The subtle differences within the required elements can make a <u>big</u>

1. As of 2007, the USDF was considering raising the requirement from 58% to 60%

difference when you are creating your own Freestyle choreography.

Since every region can develop their own lower level Freestyle classes, some areas have provided compulsory Freestyle tests along with the standard Freestyle competition.
The compulsory Freestyle test provides pre-designed choreography - the rider can choose their own music; however,
they will be judged on a predetermined pattern. On the
other hand, standard Freestyles are routines comprised of
original choreography or sequences of movements based on
the technical requirements for each level *(see previous section)*. Compulsory tests - with the exception of those areas
that provide compulsory Freestyle tests - are **not** ridden to
music. Standard Freestyles **must** be ridden with music.

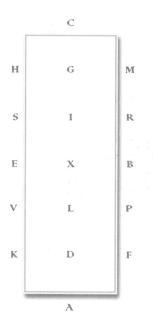

Step Three in the Process:
Know Your Rules and Requirements

First Level, Novice, or Basic Movements
Purpose:

The First Level, Novice, or Basic tests build on the foundation of the previous level by developing thrust power and achieving a degree of balance and roundness onto the bit. Each test within the level builds on the previous by adding another compulsory movement.

Sample Compulsory Movements:

1. 15m circle in a canter and lengthening of stride in the trot

2. Leg yield in the trot and lengthening of the stride in the canter

3. Change of lead through the trot

4. 10m circle at the trot and the counter canter

Example of Average Freestyle Technical Requirements:
(These requirements are based on the averages from various regions. Each country has their own set of requirements - be sure to check your local rule book).

Maximum Time - 5:00

1. **Walk** *(20m minimum continuous free walk)*

2. **10m circle in the Trot** *(both reins)*

3. **Leg Yield at the Trot** *(both reins)*

4. **Lengthening stride in the Trot** *(rising or sitting)*

5. **15m circle in the Canter** *(both reins)*

6. **Change of lead through the Trot** *(both reins*

7. **Lengthen stride in the Canter**

8. **Halts and Salutes** *(beginning and end of test)*

First, Novice, or Basic Level
Acceptable and Unacceptable Movement Chart

Acceptable	Unacceptable
Counter Canter (any configuration)	Reinback
Zigzag Leg Yield	Shoulder-In
Leg Yield Along Wall (like shoulder-n)	Travers
Lengthen Trot or Canter on a 20m circle	Renvers
Canter Serpentine	Half Pass
Simple Change	Flying Changes
Walk-Canter-Walk	Turn-on-the-Haunches
Halt-Canter-Halt-Canter	Canter or Walk Pirouette
10m Circle or Smaller at Trot	Piaffe
15m Circle or Smaller at Canter	Passage

This chart will help you to quickly identify movements that are considered above the level for competition. If you are planning on competing in a Freestyle, this is a smart and easy way to identify the movements you can or cannot use when assembling your choreography.

Step Four in the Process:
Know Your Test and Its Times

EXERCISE:

Draw out the highest test within your level using copies of the standard arena layout. Refer to the movements indicated in each box. Draw out each movement in its own separate arena *(see example below)*. Afterwards, do time estimates for each section based on the numbers you acquired in **Step One in the Process: Know Your Arena and Your Times**.

Practice the moves with the **Rhythm Riding Practice CD**.

Example:

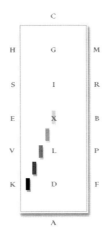

Estimated Time: 10-12 seconds
Required Move: Direction #_____ from test_____
                        K-X Leg Yield Right

Second, Elementary, or Basic Level Movements

Purpose:
Once again, these tests are adding onto the foundations of the previous ones by requiring that the horse be a little more collected. There is also increased requirements of balance, self-carriage, straightness, bending, and throughness.

Sample Compulsory Movements:

1. 10m circle in a canter; medium gaits, shoulder-in; simple change and rein back
2. Travers
3. Turn on the haunches
4. Renvers

Example of Average Freestyle Technical Requirements:
(These requirements are based on the averages from several various regions. Each country has their own set of requirements - be sure to check your local rule book).

Maximum Time - 5:00

1. **Walk** *(20m minimum continuous free walk)*

2. **Shoulder-In at the Trot** *(both reins)*

3. **Travers and or Renvers at the Trot** *(at least one must be shown on both reins)*

4. **Medium Trot**

5. **10m circle in the Canter** *(both reins)*

6. **Simple Change of lead** *(both reins)*

7. **Medium Canter**

8. **Halts and Salutes** *(beginning and end of test)*

Second, Elementary, or Basic Level
Acceptable and Unacceptable Movement Chart

Acceptable	Unacceptable
Full and Double Turn on the Haunches	Half-Pass
Medium Canter and Trot on a 20m Circle	Flying Changes
Medium Canter on the Diagonal	Canter Pirouette
10m Circle or Smaller at the Canter	Piaffe
	Passage

Third or Medium Level Movements

Purpose:

The third or medium level tests require even more collection. A clearer and more defined level of rhythmic changes along with more suppleness, balance, impulsion, and straightness.

Sample Compulsory Movements:

1. Extended gaits
2. Half-Pass at the Trot, 8m circle at the Trot
3. Single Flying Change
4. Half-Pass at the Canter
5. Release of both reins at the Canter

Example of Average Freestyle Technical Requirements:
(These requirements are based on the averages from several various regions. Each country has their own set of requirements - be sure to check your local rule book).

Maximum Time - 5:00

1. **Walk** *(20m minimum continuous extended)*
2. **Shoulder-In** *(both reins)*
3. **Trot Half Pass** *(both reins)*
4. **Extended Trot**
5. **Canter Half-Pass** *(both reins)*
6. **Counter Canter** *(both reins)*
7. **Extended Canter**
8. **Flying Changes of lead** *(both reins)*
9. **Halts and Salutes** *(beginning and end of test)*

Third or Medium Level
Acceptable and Unacceptable Movement Chart

Acceptable	Unacceptable
Everything that is not clearly forbidden	Tempi Changes 4s, 3s, 2s, 1s
Half-Pass Zigzag at the Trot	Canter Pirouette
Half-Pass Zigzag at the Canter with Flying Changes	Piaffe
Full and Double Walk Pirouettes	Passage

Fourth Level, Advanced Medium, or Medium Movements

Purpose:

 The final lower level is designed to be the transition to all of the upper level movements. At this juncture, a horse should exhibit the highest level of collection while remaining balanced and supple.

Sample Compulsory Movements:

1. Collected Walk, Walk Pirouettes
2. Very Collected Canter, Counter Change of hand in the Trot
3. Working Pirouettes in the Canter
4. 4 Tempi Changes, 3 Tempi Changes
5. Shoulder-in on the centerline
6. Half-Pirouettes in the Canter

Example of Average Freestyle Technical Requirements:
(These requirements are based on the averages from several various regions. Each country has their own set of requirements - be sure to check your local rule book).

Maximum Time - 5:00

1. **Walk** *(20m minimum continuous collected)*

2. **Walk** *(20m minimum continuous extended)*

3. **Trot Half Pass** *(both reins)*

4. **Extended Trot**

5. **Shoulder-In** *(both reins)*

6. **Canter Half-Pass** *(both reins)*

7. **Extended Canter**

8. **Flying Changes of lead every 3rd stride**
   (3 changes minimum)

9. **Canter Half-Pirouette** *(both reins)*

10. **Halts and Salutes** *(beginning and end of test)*

Fourth, Advance Medium, or Medium Level
Acceptable and Unacceptable Movement Chart

Acceptable	Unacceptable
Everything that is not clearly forbidden	Tempi Changes 2s, 1s
	Full Canter Pirouette
	Piaffe
	Passage

*"One who believes that he has mas-
tered the art of horsemanship, has
not yet begun to understand the
horse."*
Author Unknown

*"A horse in the wind -
a perfect symphony."*
Author Unknown

Dr. Cesar Parra

Dr. Cesar Parra has come a long way from his days as a Professor of Dentistry at the University of Colombia, to his well-earned ranking as one of the world's top international riders and trainers. Dr. Parra received his classical training in Germany and strongly adheres to the Classical European Training Methods taught by the old German Masters. These methods are based on the Training Scale:

Rhythm, Relaxation, Contact, Impulsion, Straightness, Collection (Takt, Losgelassenheit, Anlehnung, Schwung, Geraderichten, Versammlung)

Since his arrival in the United States in 2000, he has successfully shown at the World Cup Finals, the World Equestrian Games in Jerez, Spain and Aachen, Germany, the Olympic Games in Athens, Greece, the Pan American Games, and too many CDI competitions to mention. In 2004, he established Piaffe Performance Farms in New Jersey. In 2006, Dr. Parra won the Grand Prix Freestyle at Dressage at Devon. Along with his own successes, Dr. Parra has mentored young talents from all over the world. By imparting the wisdom of the Classical European training scale to all his students, he has managed to develop some of today's best young, up-and-coming dressage stars.

EquiChord is proud to work with and learn from Dr. Parra and his wonderful horses.

An Interview with Dr. Cesar Parra

What are the three (3) most important things you look for when you begin to put together a Freestyle?

There are three main things I always keep in mind:

1. First and foremost, that the horse is ready to show, both mentally and physically. He must have a good sense of rhythm and balance, and display the kinds of quality movements that are inherent to the level in which I'm planning to show.

2. That I have enough time to pull all the elements together for a successful performance. Practice is the key to any successful event, and I need to make sure that both the horse and I can carve out the necessary time to rehearse.

3. Listening to a lot of music. A freestyle is only as good as its components, and my efforts will be wasted if I choose the wrong kind of music for the horse's demeanor and personality.

What excites you when you are watching a well-performed Freestyle? What aspects discourage you?

I think there is nothing more wonderful to watch than a horse that is completely comfortable within the movements he's performing, coupled with music that is powerful in nature, and one that conveys a central theme. What I find discouraging is when you witness a horse that is clearly out of control or performing beyond his capabilities, or when the music has been given little attention so as to make it be little more than background music.

How have freestyles evolved or improved? What do you think about today's freestyles?

Well, they have certainly gotten better with time. I think a lot of that has to do with the expanding nature of the competitive field, and the greater exposure that international competitions have been receiving. As with any other aspect of Dressage, the more you ride and perform, the better you get. It is good to have the freedom to change things as you go along with the training, in order to hone in on the aspects that make your performance rise above the rest. There are freestyles out there today that are fantastic; really, really good. They are introducing new music and choreographic styles that are doing a lot of good for the sport.

Do you see any differences between the United States and Europe in regards to musical freestyles? If so, what do you consider the most important aspects to be?

In every single aspect, the sport is generally more developed in Europe than in the United States. It is more popular amongst the general population, and thus it is easier for European riders to gather more sponsors. The more popular the sport and the more sponsors you acquire, the more competitions there are bound to exist. This scenario forces the riders to do their best at developing better and more unique musical freestyles. For me, the greatest differences are that European riders bring along better musical recordings, and better choreographed routines. The key to their success in the field also pertains to the quality they display through all the levels, from their riding to the music.

Do you think that freestyles will one day become a mandatory part of lower level competition? Explain your reasons, either pro or con.

I do not think so. Mainly, because I do not believe that there is not enough established technique for freestyles in the lower levels. Many people tend to look at the freestyle as something that is fun to do, so they will go to a show and compete without first developing the proper technique. In the long run, they develop bad performance habits that will

41

do them more harm than good as they advance in their development. Regardless of how you may feel about the art, you still need a good technique in order to show a good freestyle.

What do you see as the future of freestyles?

I think that we are going to start to see much more creativity coming into the mix. With the advancements in portable recording technologies, I can envision people doing recordings with live musical instrumentation, perhaps using a whole band or even introducing their own original pieces.

When you're in the process of riding a freestyle, what goes through your mind? How would you categorize your experience when you and your horse are "in the zone"?

I love to ride my horse to the music I've selected. Regardless of where I am in the ring, I follow the music; I feel a certain unity with the horse through our combined rhythms. In competition, I love riding to music because the general freedom the test allows gives me an opportunity to score more points.

"Rhythm is the most elemental component of riding. No matter what level you are riding, it is necessary to establish a good rhythm in the beginning. A lack of consistent rhythm will become readily apparent as one moves up through the levels. Without rhythm, you will never be able to piaffe or passage correctly."

~ Dr. Cesar Parra

Chapter Two
Rhythm and Riding

"Music and Rhythm find their way into the secret places of the soul"
Plato

The word *"rhythm"* is predominantly seen throughout the various definitions of dressage, and is the foundation of everything we do. That being said, there is no better time to introduce music than at the beginning of the training cycle of a horse and/or rider. With the assistance of practice music that contains a consistent beat that matches the average beats for each gait, the horse and rider will find the support needed to help maintain a steady tempo.

Introduction
Our lives are, quite literally, driven by rhythm. Our bodies not only guide themselves by the inner beat of our heart, but through the endless rhythmic patterns we expose ourselves to on a daily basis. From a favorite song on the radio to the subliminal tapping of our car's tires as we streak down the highway, rhythm is the elemental force that dictates the pace at which each moment of our lives is conducted. Amongst the myriad creatures in the animal kingdom, horses possess one of Nature's most sensitive and discriminating sense of rhythm. Anyone who has ridden on a horse will attest to the unique bond that exists when horse and rider begin to share a common rhythm through any given gait. The horse's hypersensitivity to its surroundings *(to include the very heartbeat of its rider)* sets in motion a palpable rhythm that is truly one of the

most profound experiences any human can share with another creature on this earth. When you introduce the emotional simplicity of music to the mix, the bond is further heightened by the language of notes and cadences; waves and patterns. The very nature of music is to translate into sound the same emotional and rhythmic patterns that flow through us on a daily basis. When you're able to find that symbiotic tonality with your horse, the relationship is elevated to a greater sense of respect and understanding.

 "Rhythm" comes from the Greek word **rhythmos,** *which means "measured flow or movement, rhythm". Writings on the nature of rhythm in music can be traced back to such luminaries as the Greek philosopher Aristoxenus from the 4th century B.C.*

Understanding Rhythm

Speaking of understanding, let's begin by looking into the nature of rhythm as a whole. Don't worry - we're not going to pull out a music theory book, nor will we subject you to an impromptu lesson on Hindemith's rhythmic methodologies *(the insatiably curious will just have to adapt).* Let's start by looking at the definition of the word itself:

Webster's Dictionary Definition

rhythm | ˈriðəm| | ˌrɪðəm| | ˌrɪð(ə)m|
noun
1 a: an ordered recurrent alternation of strong and weak elements in the flow of sound and silence in speech
2 a: the aspect of music comprising all the elements *(as accent, meter, and tempo)* that relate to forward movement
3 a: movement, fluctuation, or variation marked by the regular recurrence or natural flow of related elements

ORIGIN mid 16th cent. *(also originally in the sense [rhyme]): from French* **rhythme,** *or via Latin from Greek* **rhuthmos** *(related to* **rhein 'to flow').**

The first of these descriptions relates to the manner in which we communicate verbally using inflections, pauses, and streams of words to create a repetitive pattern in our speech. Some of the more common examples are those folks who use public speaking as part of their trade such as auctioneers, motivational speakers, and politicians. In today's music field, the more commonly known form of this pattern relates to various styles of rap music, where the emphasis is placed on the rhythmic patterns of words more so than on the underlying melody itself.

Now, in the second description for **rhythm** noted previously, it referred to *"accent, meter, and tempo"* as those aspects of music that relate to its forward movement. Let's park our thoughts on this for a spell, as it contains the very heart of our search for the meaning of rhythm. We'll first look at their definitions as set forth within the musical world, and then expand on each in regards to their relevance within the world of musical freestyles.

Author's Note: *The following descriptions employ the use of some terms that may only be familiar to those with a rudimentary knowledge of music theory. If you would like to take a look at a simple primer on musical terminology, please refer to* **Appendix 2: Music Terminology 101 - A VERY Short Primer on Musical Notation** *located at the end of this book. It may not help you to sing on key, but the explanations contained therein may help shed some light on the subject.*

Accent is defined as:
"a greater stress given to one musical tone than to its neighbors"

It provides an aide by which we mark the phrasing of a particular rhythm. For example: If you've ever watched a group

45

of people engaged in marching *(be it for a parade, military procession, or even a marching band)*, you will sometimes hear a cadence called out as "HUP-two-three-four, HUP-two-three-four..." In this instance, we have a cadence of four beats with the emphasis - or accent - on the first. Another example is when you're counting a canter stride; the down-beat occurs when the inside foreleg hits the ground.

Meter is defined as:

"the basic recurrent rhythmical pattern of note values, accents, and beats per measure in music"

It's what indicates the beat within a given pattern or cadence. For example, let's say that the marching band we saw earlier needed to perform in a large assembly, and could not rely on someone calling out the cadence. By telling each band member that they are to march to a 4/4 meter, they would know how many beats are in each bar *(four)*, and what the notation is for each beat *(in this case, one quarter note per beat)*. When measuring a horse's "pure" walk *(i.e. when he/she is striding with a distinctive 4-beat count)*, the gait they're performing is a perfect example of a 4/4 meter.

Tempo is defined as:

"the rate of speed of a musical piece or passage indicated by one of a series of directions (as largo, presto, or allegro) and often by an exact metronome marking"

This rounds out the road map for any piece of music. As the **meter** helps to indicate the beat and the **accent** gives us the phrasing, **tempo** gives us the speed at which the piece of music is to be performed. As noted in the definition, musicians define the speed of different segments of music through a series of directives written in Italian. Case in point: In the body of the definition shown, **largo** means "long", and is interpreted with a slow, pensive beat. **Presto** means, "fast", and is interpreted as such. **Allegro** means

46

"happy", and usually translates musically into a spry, lively beat. You may also encounter such terms as **adagio** *(slow and stately)*, **andante** *(walking pace)*, **allegro con moto** *(lively, with movement)*, and **vivace** *(vibrant or lively - more so than allegro)*. In the equestrian world, the tempo at which music is played is guided by your horse's gait - and that, in turn, is measured by how many BPMs *(**B**eats **P**er **M**inute)* your horse covers in a given timeframe. Let's say that you count off your horse's walk by noting when each of his *(or her)* front hooves strikes the arena floor. Begin tracking to the left, using the front left leg as the accent or downbeat, and continue to count each front footfall for one full minute. When the time has elapsed, you may find that you've counted 98 strikes *(each horse has its own speed - this is merely an example of an average count for one horse)*. That gives you the tempo for your horse's walk.

We're sure you noticed how we snuck in that little tidbit on BPMs. Well, we'll get to that in just a moment. Right now, let's take a quick recap of what we've seen on the nature of rhythm, and its importance in your musical world.

Rhythm is the beat by which all things move. Its forward motion is dependent on the speed *(tempo)*, pattern *(meter)*, and phrasing *(accent)* of a given beat - mainly that of your horse's gait. Rhythm is not dependent on a melody, nor is a melody dependent on rhythm - they are each a unique entity whose collaborative efforts bring forth the plethora of music we hear today. Whether classical or country, abstract or zydeco, rhythm is the foundation through which music finds its heartbeat, and the tool through which you and your horse can develop a deeper sense of togetherness.

Step Five in the Process:
Hear the Beat

 Unmounted Exercise: In this exercise, we're going to try and find five (5) examples of a rhythm, but without resorting to music or drums. We want you to look around where you happen to be at - whether it's your house, barn, arena, office, or car - and we want you to listen for a sound *(no matter how simple you may initially think it to be)* and find its rhythm by clapping your hands *(or tapping your fingers)* along with it. We'll give you some easy examples: A washing machine; a copier machine; your car's blinker; a dishwasher. Shakespeare once said, "the earth has music for those who listen". Rhythms are no different - have fun!

Putting It All Together

Now let's put all this knowledge to work! In the previous segment, we saw how you can determine a tempo by counting the steps your horse takes during a given gait. In our example, we saw that the horse's walk had a tempo of *98 BPMs*. **BPMs**, or **B**eats **P**er **M**inute, are nothing more than a way to measure the speed *(or **tempo**)* at which a piece of music is moving. With the aid of a metronome, this measurement can be acquired with greater accuracy and in much less time. Incidentally, a **metronome**, for the sake of simplicity, is nothing more than a musical stopwatch. There are numerous models whose features, like Swiss Army knives, often exceeds the needs of the average person looking to simply measure BPMs. The one feature that is a "must have" is the ability to vary the BPMs per one (1) beat increments. Because a vast majority of music out there *(whether classical or hip-hop)* adhere to a given set of speeds, many metronomes only offer tempo changes through a variety of predefined settings *(some typical examples are: 60, 72, 80, 88,*

100, 120). Although the range can be sizable, it still does not offer much help if you need to find a speed of, let us say, 143. So, make sure that the metronome you're planning to buy has a tempo/value adjustment that moves in increments of one (1) beat per measure. See **Appendix 3: Choosing a Metronome** for more information on basic models, features, and pricing.

Now, back to BPMs. In order to match a piece of music to your horse, you first need to measure the BPMs for your horse's various gaits. Although these will vary from one horse to another due to size, confirmation, and personality, the average speeds for each gait that you will generally measure are:

Average BPM Chart

Average BPMs	Small	Medium	Large
Walk	103	98	96
Trot	158	152	148
Canter	105	100	98

The **Rhythm Riding Practice CD** that accompanies this book follows the averages noted in this table. Keep in mind, each horse's gait is going to be slightly different, so do not assume that Private Dancer over there is going to have a BPM of 100 for his walk just because your best friend's horse *(who, by the way, happens to be your Pas De Deux companion)* has the same gait. Another reason to measure your BPMs is to avoid the infamous assumption issue - just because a horse is of a given height and weight is no indicator as to what his or her BPMs should be. We had a situation once where a 17hh warmblood *(who weighed in at about 1,600lbs/727kgs)* was assumed to have slower gaits due to his imposing size. When we got him into the arena for testing - well, let's put it this way, we had three people confirm the results, because his BPMs were registering as those of a large pony. Although he was quite a behemoth to behold, his gaits were that of a lithe ballerina. Remember: **When it comes to BPMs, assumptions are the weaker side of accuracy**. Another thing to keep is mind is that, although no horse is ever going to keep perfect synchronization to a piece of music all the time, it is important to know your horse's gaits to ensure that the musical match is approximated as best as possible. Not only does this come in handy for your freestyle, but it makes for a helpful reference guide when measuring your routine within the arena, and makes the selection of a Pas De Deux or Quadrille partners that much easier and exacting.

Step Six in the Process:
Know Your BPMs

OK, you're now armed with your nifty metronome, and are ready to measure your BPMs at the walk, trot, and canter. You hand the metronome to an observer on the ground; you mount your horse, and ask the observer to start counting. Right? Well, "yes" and "no". Although measuring the BPMs is simply a matter of counting steps, you need to ensure that the right combination of steps are being counted correctly and in the right sequence in order to get a useable BPM. The following page contains a simple guide to help you gauge your horse's steps:

Measuring BPMs	Walk	Trot	Canter
What to watch for	Each footfall; use the front left hoof as your downbeat.	Front left leg and rear right leg strike the ground simultaneously, followed by the same motion on the opposite sides	The front left leg and the right hind leg strike simultaneously, then the front right leg, followed by a short suspension, then the left hind strikes, and the pattern repeats.
What to listen for	A steady 4-beat count	A steady 2-beat count	A quick 3-beat count, followed by a singular "thump"; sounds like a short, 3-beat drum roll immediately followed by a short bass drum hit *(brum-dah-dah....boom)*
What to count	Each footfall	Count the two front hoof strikes or two rear hoof strikes in a left-right fashion	The reaching stride of the inside fore-leg as the down-beat.
How many steps per grouping	4	2	1

51

One of the easiest ways to measure the BPMs at the rising trot is to watch the rider's body while posting up or down *("up" being one beat, and "down" being the second beat)*. Another way is to watch the rider's hips at the sitting trot as they follow the horse's movement. If you want to see if the horse is following the beat, simply watch their tail as it moves to and fro to the rhythm of the music!

In the preceding table, the last entry talks about "steps per grouping". If you had a chance to look at **Appendix 2** regarding musical notation, you may recall our explanation for bars *(or measures)*. In music *(as in dance)*, musical phrasing is measured by a grouping of bars. Musical notes are arranged *(as are words)* to create sentences or, in musical parlance, phrases. Musicians tend to mark phrases in groups of two or four *(though there are a wide variety of styles)*, whereas dancers mark their phrasing in groups of eight. If you've ever seen a film or TV show where they depict dancers at a rehearsal, you'll invariably hear someone counting off, "...and five, six, seven, eight!", and the whole ensemble will begin to dance. Musicians? Well, they take the shortcut by counting off, "...two, three, four". This will be of use to you when assembling your freestyle, as it will help to train your ear to hear musical "sentences" that complete a given phrase or movement. The one thing that contributes most to the "radio dial" effect in freestyles is musical selections whose phrases are not allowed to cycle through before moving on to the next phrase. Like listening to a conversation filled with half sentences, the experience becomes either boring or irritating - two responses best avoided when assembling a winning freestyle.

Armed with these small but significant tidbits of information, you can begin to explore musical selections that will fit your horse's gaits and, through the use of accents, tempos, and meter, you can further discover new rhythms and styles that will suit your personality and that of your horse.

Riding to Rhythms

 You're now in possession of some solid pieces of information that will give you an edge as you venture forth into the wonderfully rewarding field of musical dressage *(or Kür)*. But, what about you? As a rider, we're sure that you are already starting to think about how to translate your knowledge into practical guidelines for being in the saddle, but where to begin? One of the easiest ways to make the transition is to think of your body as an instrument. Better yet, think of both you **and** your horse as a singular instrument. Take the violin, for example. It is a wonderful instrument, diverse in sound and use. Although it is considered a stringed instrument of singular construction, it also has a bow. These two separate entities work together to create the distinctive sounds we have come to know and love. The violin creates its sound from within the core of the instrument, much like you *(as a rider)* must initiate your moves from your core group of muscles. Like the bow, you convey your wishes on top of your horse with your legs, core, and hips in very specific yet subtle ways in order to move your horse forward in the arena. One without the other is merely a part of the equation and, like the bow and violin, can only create that magic by working in a collaborative environment.

Following this train of thought, let's look at you and your horse as that collective instrument. No musical instrument is played through sheer brute force alone; it is the strong yet well-controlled movements of key muscles and joints that help elicit the sounds that emanate from each instrument. The same applies to you and your horse - the subtle movements you both achieve as part of a routine or Kür are not executed through a battle of wills, but from the firmness and conviction of a collaborative effort. A horse is only as good as the instructions he/she receives, and responds best when there's a sense of respect and collaboration. Remember: What you are trying to achieve in a freestyle is the creation of a performance piece - not simply a rote routine that happens to have music as a backdrop. Properly trained horses don't react for the sake of movement, nor do they run for the

sake of flight. They do so because of what they are, and because of what each act represents to their own essence.
That's what you need to infuse into your freestyle in order to
create a visual work of art. You need to execute each move
for the sake of representing something beyond the mere act
of movement. You must elevate the routine from a series of
actions to a sublime representation of poetry in motion.
Once you and your horse have established that symbiotic
relationship, you both have to integrate the rhythmic aspects
of the music into the performance to complete the cycle.
Remember how rhythm is the integration of accent, meter,
and tempo? So goes the Kür; it's the seamless integration of
rider, horse, and music.

Step Seven in the Process:
Hear the Beat - Part Two
EXERCISES:
Group Mounted Exercises:

 In this exercise, it's the folks on the ground who are being tested. Elect a member of your group to ride in an arena while the rest of you gather along the perimeter. The rider will perform a series of gaits while the spectators listen to the rides with their eyes closed. The exercise here is to see if you can hear what gait is being performed. Count off the steps as you hear them, and see how many of you are on the same beat.

While the one person is riding in the arena, have the folks on the ground count off the beats to see if everyone is on the same beat. Try it during a freestyle to see if the horse and rider stick to the varied beats within the performance.

Group Unmounted Exercises:
Get a group member to clap a rhythm - be creative and try different variations. Then, have the rest of the group try and determine the BPM just by listening, while one uses a metronome to confirm the tempo. See if you can begin to train your ears to approximate different BPMs. While listening to a piece of music, count off the phrases in segments of eight beats; find the downbeat in each grouping.

Advanced Exercise:
Using the **Rhythm Riding Practice CD**, ride your horse to one of the slower or faster BPM segments, and influence him *(or her)* to fit the beat.

Points to Ponder:
Acronyms are always useful in helping us remember key points of a routine or exercise. Use this phrase to remember the essential rhythmic components of the freestyle:

Always use the **RIGHT FORMAT** when training for a Kür -

RIGHT: Rhythm **I**nspires **G**reat **H**orse **T**raining
FORMAT: Focus **O**n **R**emembering **M**eter, **A**ccent & **T**empo

Chapter Three
Busta' Move

> *"The dance is a poem of which each*
> *movement is a word."*
> **Mata Hari**

Riding the Warm-Up

Now that you are equipped with all the knowledge you gained in the first two chapters, you are going to start putting it to use. The process of musical riding will now begin by utilizing the **Rhythm Riding Practice CD**. Once again, here is how the CD is formatted: The first section is the warm-up and practice session. It is approximately 22 minutes long, depending on the section you choose. The warm up repeats three times, each time with different average BPMs. They follow our average BPM chart:

Average BPMs	Small	Medium	Large
Walk	103	98	96
Trot	158	152	148
Canter	105	100	98

This is your time to have fun and experiment. Set aside a planned training day that is dedicated solely to developing your musical riding skills. Since you have found your average BPMs, fit your ride to one of the sections of the CD that most closely matches your horse. For example, if you found that your average trot BPM is 150, try riding the warm up section for both the medium and large horse. Hearing the rhythm and staying with it are the goals of this basic CD; trying different rhythms is a great exercise. Since walk and canter BPMs can be very close, try cantering during the walk portions and walking during the canter portions. After you have practiced with the CD for a while, record your BPMs again. This will help to further hone in on your average BPMs, allowing you to become very precise when it comes time to create an original Freestyle. You will find that your BPMs will change depending on several factors, including your increased ability to relax and stay consistent with a beat.

Freestyles could become a required part of competition at all levels. Regardless of its status, performing a Freestyle is fun, rewarding, and assists in technical instruction. Sit down with your trainer and formulate a training plan that includes the development of your musical riding skills. There are many trainers out there who embrace this element and are looking for their students to express an interest. Share the process and continue to develop your technical skills along with your musical skills; choose a specific day to practice your musical rides. You are building upon the foundation of your technique; on the days you choose to ride with music, your focus should be on developing those musical skills. Therefore, your goal at first is to relax and simply focus on maintaining a steady rhythm while carrying your horse within the appropriate frame for your level or, better yet, one level below. Ride at the technical level at which you feel very comfortable. As your musical skills become second nature, your basic technical foundation will begin to build as well. The longer you practice to the CD and develop patterns, the more attuned you will become to your horse's strengths and weaknesses. Does he need more impulsion? Does he need to relax? Is he stiffer on one side or the other? As you experiment with the different rhythmic sections of the CD, you may find that your horse canters more comfortably to the right at the average BPM for a larger horse, whereas he canters more comfortably to the left at the average BPM for a medium horse. Share these observations with your trainer. He or she may suggest some exercises or techniques to help even-out the rhythm, or there may be a physical issue that needs to be addressed. This is your time to experiment and have fun. Start listening to other types of music and find out what inspires you. Don't get too concerned about what is right or wrong. These are your practice sessions of discovery. Beginning to answer these questions will help you develop a musical understanding for those types of music that will best suit you and your partner, as well as where and how certain movements need to be placed within the choreography to best showcase your ride. Find the places and moments in the music that are right for you and your partner, and build your patterns around them.

Step Eight in the Process:
Sway

EXERCISE: At the Walk

Feel the sway of your hips in time with the music. At first, don't try to influence your horse to stay in beat, but rather walk a nice, free walk. If you feel comfortable, take your feet out of the stirrups and let your body feel the rhythm. Start counting aloud or to yourself to the motion of your hips. It will actually be a 1 -2, 1-2, rhythm as your horse's hips rise and fall. If you feel yourself tuning out the music, STOP and realign. Part of this exercise is to train you to hear the music and follow the beat, not tune it out. Repeat the exercise at the trot and the canter using the beat exercises from the previous chapter.

Developing Patterns

When dance choreographers begin to develop a performance, they are generally inspired by a piece of music first.
From that inspiration, they begin to listen to the music re-
peatedly until they see the completed dance unfold in their
mind's eye. The music dictates the movement more often
than the movement dictates the music. More often than not
in our work, we are assigned the task of making the music fit
the movements. Freestyles are often a last minute after-
thought, with the music trailing behind as the final consideration. The choreography for a ride is developed before a
specific piece of music has been chosen. We are then sent a
list of musical selections that don't necessarily fit the BPMs
or style of the ride or partners, and it is up to us as arrangers
to piece everything together and underscore the ride. In this
instance, we are using the word *underscoring* to mean the
addition of a piece of music to an existing work, such as the
scoring of a movie. Generally, when a movie is completed,
it is sent to the composer or arranger for them to add the
music underneath the action. Although this can be done effectively for Freestyles, it is akin to putting the cart before the
horse. That being said, we would like to begin teaching the
choreographic process in a more artistically traditional fashion by starting with the music first - or at least the idea of the
music first.

As you may have observed, we did not devise choreography
for the practice portion of the CD. Instead, we hope that you
will experiment with your own movements and patterns to
build choreography that is your own. Start by introducing
yourself to the music; listen to it both in and out of the saddle. Feel how the music moves your body with the beat.
The movement will flow out of the sound, into your body,
and into your horse. That is the organic development of the
choreography. Try this with every piece of music you hear
and see if you can visualize different patterns. The more you
are inspired by a piece of music, the more imaginative you

will become. Give yourself the opportunity to become good friends with the music within the **Rhythm Riding Practice CD**, and create your practice routine from there.

Until you get to know the music fairly well, ride with it in a relaxed, free-form manner. Listen for the transitions, the climaxes, and specifically the beat changes. Play with different movements and patterns until you find one that fits particularly well with a portion of the music; let it tell you what to do next. For example, you may be riding a three loop serpentine at the trot and, just as you are doing your diagonal and bend change, the music seems to magically support that movement. In that instant, you, the movement, and your horse have blended seamlessly with the music to become one. Once you feel that incredible sensation, you will want to recreate it over and over again. When it comes time for you to develop a Freestyle from scratch, it should be crafted from a series of those special moments, strung together like a pearl necklace. Each movement should flow to the next in a relaxed, easy fashion with the music seamlessly blending them together so you may visualize the choreography every time you hear the music. Look for those moments within the **Rhythm Riding Practice CD** and draw the patterns out on a piece of paper using the arena template. Each time you find a segment like that, draw it out until you have created a full routine for your practice session. One will build upon the other until you have crafted an entire session that you can ride with ease.

Step Nine in the Process:
See the Music

Draw out your exercise patterns on an arena template. Do each pattern on a separate piece of paper and assign approximate times based on the timing exercise from the previous chapter. From the patterns you have created, start constructing a routine. You can lay your patterns out on a desk or the floor, and play around by rearranging them in different sequences. Try various and unusual combinations and see how they fit with the music. You will train yourself to a point where you can hear a phrase of music, or craft a section of choreography and know how long it will take to complete, as well as how much of the arena it will cover.

In the dance world, it is often said that a true artist dances the steps in between and a circus performer moves from "trick" to "trick". What does that mean? In essence, a choreographed routine can be seen as a series of "tricks" - one grouping of movements followed by another. The preparatory steps are there just to get the dancer, gymnast, skater, or rider set up for the next "trick". In dance, the "tricks" could be a set of turns followed by a show of balance. In riding, it could be a piaffe followed by an extended trot. In each, there are preparatory movements that happen in between. A good example is to watch a gymnast. Each time they are about to execute a tumbling run, they stand in a corner, focus intensely, lift up onto the balls of their feet, inhale, and off they go!

In any well-executed choreography carried out by someone who truly understands and analyzes their performance, the movements in between - the transitions - carry as much, if not more weight than the "trick". They are the threads that smoothly weave the work together. Without them, the ride cannot exist. In any well performed Freestyle, the rider pays close attention to every hoof step; each is precisely timed and planned. Riders such as Anky van Grunsven truly grasp this concept, and perfectly construct their rides so they make sense and are complete pieces - not merely disjointed "tricks" with background music.

Step Ten in the Process:

Fill the Spaces in Between

Once you have developed a section of your practice routine, start working on the nuances. Time the transitions smoothly with the music, making sure you hit the musical marks you have designated for each section. Start counting out your pattern in segments of 8 beats; that will help you learn the phrasing, especially when the beats change. The more fluent you become with identifying the beats and phrases, the better you will be able to hear the proper construction of a Freestyle. It is advisable that you have your trainer watch you at this point to help you from the ground.

Riding with the Music - Not in Spite of It

At this point, a further explanation of this title is in order. When you are riding in spite of the music, there is no fully realized connection between the horse/rider partnership and the music. The music is merely playing in the background at one rhythm while the rider is detached, focusing solely on the pattern or technique and completely ignoring what is transpiring musically. Having music accompany your daily practice sessions is a wonderful and refreshing thing. It takes the edge off of a tough day and makes a mundane training session fun. Unfortunately, there can be a negative side.

The average off-the-shelf CD most likely does not have any substantial portions whose BPMs are even close to riding averages. For example, most pop music runs between 115-124 BPMs, whereas dance or electronic music is generally set in the 130s, and jazz is between 100 and 115. Obviously, these are sweeping generalizations; nevertheless, the message is that it is important to carefully pick the music that accompanies your ride. When the music doesn't match your horse's BPMs, your natural instinct is to block out the music and focus on the task at hand. In essence, you are teaching your brain and your body to dismiss the music. As with any other neuromuscular activity, the more you practice a movement, the more your muscles will remember it. The same applies to the music. When you become accustomed to finding the rhythm within the music and staying with it, in time, your body will innately follow the rhythm at hand.

Horses are naturally blessed with that instinctual rhythm. We have always been amazed to observe how most of the horses we work with pick up the beat and stay with it - even when we purposely change it. They will cock their ears back, listen, process the new beat, then do their best to stay with it - sometimes even when the rider doesn't hear it. In fact, they can get downright adamant about the choreography. We were doing a First or Novice Level piece where the horse was to perform a simple downward transition from the canter to the trot. This particular horse loved his canter music! We had the music transitioning dramatically into the final trot sequence. As the music swelled, the rider had choreographed the transition across the short diagonal. Well, this horse didn't concur with that assessment. He felt he should canter across the short diagonal and do the transition afterwards. You know what? He was right! It was by far a more powerful transition and truly expressed the mood of the music. Never discount your horse's input; trust their instincts and build that partnership with them throughout this process. Who knows? Their choices may surprise you.

Step Eleven in the Process:
Musical BPMs

Exercise:
Musical BPMs

 The goal of this exercise is for you to become accustomed to picking up on the music that fits your horse's BPMs. Since you established your horse's tempos using the exercises in the previous chapters, you know the rhythmic pattern your horse follows. Take your metronome and set it to tick at the beat of your horse's walk and start tapping that beat out on your leg. Repeat with the Trot and the Canter, and try to remember those tempos. Now, play several different types of music and see if you can find selections that are close to your horse's natural rhythm. This may be more challenging than it sounds - some music can fool you! Once you become comfortable with this process, you'll be able to listen to most music and feel if it fits.

In order to ride with the music instead of in spite of it, it is best to set aside a specific day where you will be riding with music that fits your BPMs - or at least approximates them, and your focus is on hearing the music and following it's transitions.

Relax and Have Fun!

The most important thing about riding with the music is to relax and have fun. Music can transport you to other times and places. It can lift your spirits when you are down, or make you weep. The music we produced for the **Rhythm Riding Practice CD** was designed to allow you to clearly hear the beat, and to encourage relaxation. With that said, we have adapted some traditional warm-up exercises for riders in order to further enforce focusing on the beat and relaxation.

If you have some basic exercises that you do to warm up in the saddle, practice them with the CD. During the initial walking portion of the CD, do some simple stretches and relaxation exercises in time with the music. There are several instructional tools on the market that have adapted Pilates, Yoga, or Tai Chi exercises for equestrians. Take the preliminary exercises from any of these disciplines and incorporate them into your musical warm-up. Remember to do them in time with the music - first in real time and then at half time. Really listen to the music and feel the beat in your movement. If you don't have any specific exercises, we have assembled some very basic relaxation exercises on the following pages that will not only help you warm up, but also reinforce the beat of the music.

Step Twelve in the Process:
Just Breathe

Exercises:
Just Breathe

 Practice doing these breathing exercises while you are at the walk. Take in a slow, deep breath through your nose, and slowly release it through your mouth. Find the beat in the music and inhale for 4 counts and exhale for 4 counts. Whenever you find yourself building tension or holding your breath, take in a deep breath and release.

Place the reins in one hand and place your other hand on your abdomen. Repeat the exercise. Inhale through your nose for 4 counts and release the breath through your mouth for 4 counts. Feel your abdomen rise and fall with each breath. If you feel your chest rising and falling with the breath instead of your abdomen, you are holding tension in your upper body and not fully utilizing your core muscles.

Taking both reins again, inhale for 4 counts and feel the breath expand your back in between both of your shoulder blades. Exhale for 4 counts. Alternate feeling your abdomen rise and fall with the slow breaths, and your back open and close with the slow breaths.

Step Thirteen in the Process:
On a Roll

Exercises
On a Roll

1. Start by taking your right foot out of the stirrup. Start circling it in a clockwise direction. Do the circles in a relaxed and smooth motion. Repeat the clockwise circles 8 times, keeping it time with the music *(1-2, 1-2)*. Take the two counts to complete the circle. For example, if you are looking at the face of a clock, the "one" beat would be at "6" on the clock face and "two" would be at the "12" on the clock face. Repeat the series of 8 counter-clockwise.

2. Repeat the exercise above at half time *(1-2-3-4-, 1-2-3-4)*, taking a full 4 counts to complete the rotation. This time you will take twice as long to go around the clock face. The "one" beat would be at the "3" on the clock, the "two" beat would be at "6", the "three" beat would be at "9" and the "four" would be at "12". Do a series of 4. Remember, it will take you twice as long to do the half time circles as it will to do the real time circles.

Repeat exercises one and two with your left foot.

3. Repeat exercise one and two with each wrist. Take your reins in one hand freeing the other and do the circle combinations listed above.

4. Keeping the reins in your left hand, do shoulder rolls at half time with your right shoulder *(1-2-3-4, 1-2-3-4)*. Switch your reins to the right hand and repeat the shoulder exercise on the left.

5. Do head rolls starting to the right, taking a full 8 count to complete the movement. Remember the clock face and visualize reaching the 6 on the clock when you are on the "four" beat and reaching 12 on the clock when you are on the "eight" beat.

Step Fourteen in the Process:
Head and Neck Stretch

Find a neutral head position where you are looking straight ahead, the back of your neck is long, and your chin is parallel to the ground. Keep you chin level and elongate your back and neck even more. Feel the spaces between each vertebrae and lengthen them. Stretch your legs down to the ground by making the space in your hips longer. As you reach down to the ground, feel as though someone has you by the ankles and is gently pulling your legs to meet the ground while another is lifting you up by an imaginary string attached to the top of your head - just like the strings on a marionette. Lengthen your neck and back without tilting your head. Remember to keep your chin parallel to the ground at all times. After you have lengthened, pull your chin back as if to touch it to your spine. Contract your chin back for two counts and release for two counts. Repeat 8 times.

Nicole Uphoff-Selke

Nicole's deep love of horses began when she was nine years old. The double individual Olympic gold medalist began riding daily treks across the dunes of the North Sea island of Sylt. A year later, her parents presented her with her first horse *(Waldfee)* on her tenth birthday, and she began her lessons in earnest. Her first riding instructor was Cavalry Captain Willi Korioth from Kaarst. Two years later, she moved to Duisburg where she continued her training under the tutelage of Antonius Holland. There she started to excel at show jumping and dressage events up to Class L *(elementary).*

A year later, her father presented her with two geldings - Askan, then six years old, and a three-year old brown Westphalian named Rembrandt. Both horses were ridden and trained by Nicole, who was now fourteen years old, and still under the watchful eyes of Antonius Holland.

In 1988, she won the German Dressage Championship, followed by the overwhelming and sensational individual double gold success at the 1988 Olympic Games in Seoul. The 1992 Olympic Games in Barcelona brought her a repetition of the success in Seoul, gathering two additional gold medals riding her favorite son, Rembrandt, and thus solidifying her status as one of the most successful riders in international dressage.

EquiChord was honored to spend time with Nicole during one of her many visits to the United States, and to share her views concerning the nature of freestyles in today's competitive arena.

An Interview with Nicole Uphoff-Selke

We understand that you initially did not like freestyles - explain to us exactly why that was the case?

Well for me - and I think it's the same for a lot of people - I always felt that it was very hard to put a freestyle together. In most cases *(for upper levels)*, you can only have a six-minute routine and, if it's too long or too short, you have to re-work it until everything fits - and that can take ages. Sometimes, you'll write something down at home for your routine and you think, "wow I have it!" This is not exactly easy; and then when you ride to it, you discover that you're five seconds too long. Suddenly, you find yourself thinking, "where can I cut from; how can I make it shorter?" You attempt to take something out, only to realize that you'll have to re-write everything because now you're on the wrong hand or whatever. This process can takes ages, and that is exactly what I hated. When everything was finally done, it was fun to ride! But to get there, the process is awfully tedious. There's always the worry of taking care of your horse, but you still have to practice long and hard to perfect the freestyle routine. Many people across all levels still do not take this very seriously; they take music from other riders, then try to put something together just prior to a show. You cannot ride someone's music with another horse because the gaits will be all wrong, so there's no sense in doing that. One way or another, these discrepancies will show up in the arena.

Where do you think freestyles are going, and why?

I don't think they can go much further, because the freestyle is already very important in competitive circles. As we started to make the freestyle more popular, we looked for ways to introduce it into the classical aspects of dressage - you cannot get it to be more important than that. Because of this, I believe that attendance has improved. I mean, when I do commentaries for these types of shows - the smaller ones, not international - the audience area is packed when they advertise that I'll be commenting on the freestyle rides. I think this happens because people are interested in this kind of venue where there are freestyles plus commentary; they love it, even in the small shows of 500 or 600 people. I think many see it as sport plus fun.

In your opinion, what kind of information do riders need most in terms of the freestyle process and ways to make it better?

I think that people need to spend more time developing an ear for music as it relates to rhythm. For me, it's difficult sometimes to hear if a piece of music is right for a trot or canter. Some people have a natural ability to hear different musical selections and know how they fit to the various gaits, while others do not have an innate ear for music. I think that many riders misinterpret the rhythms in a piece of music when compared against a horse's natural beat. When freestyles are improperly performed because of an obvious disconnect between the music and the horse, that deficiency will show up in the arena. I also feel that choreography is another big hurdle for people. I mean, I see a lot of freestyles, but it's hard to remember each requirement and come up with really good ideas for patterns.

When you put a freestyle together, how do you approach your music as part of the process?

I start with the choreography first. I don't hear a piece of music and think of it as fitting a particular move like a pirouette or passage. I just know that I would like to use it in a freestyle, so I hand it over to the professionals to cut it in the studio to fit the choreography. Once I have my music, I listen to it all the time with a recorder and headphones. After a while, if you listen very carefully, you will understand and recognize every movement, every nuance of the piece. It becomes a part of you - when you are riding, the music will tell you exactly where you are. If you want to be really good, you have to do it like this - it's a big thing for me.

72

Chapter Four

Putting It All Together

"Riding a horse is not a gentle hobby, to be picked up and laid down like a game of Solitaire. It is a grand passion."
Ralph Waldo Emerson

Choreography
Definition:

choreography | ˌkôrēˈägrəfē| |ˈkɔriˌɑgrəfi| |ˈkɒrɪˌɒgrəfi|
noun
the sequence of steps and movements in dance or figure skating, esp. in a ballet or other staged dance.
• the art or practice of designing such sequences.
• the written notation for such a sequence.

ORIGIN late 18th cent. (in the sense [written notation of dancing]): from Greek *khoreia 'dancing in unison'* (from *khoros 'chorus'*) + **-graphy**.

Although the term "choreography" has ancient origins, it's actual introduction into our vernacular is relatively recent; it was not added to the American Dictionary until 1950. Prior to then, movement sequences were credited as *dances* or *staged ensembles*. The expansion of the term was highly influenced by the films of the day, and the mid-20th century surge of groundbreaking new choreographers such as Agnes De Mille, Martha Graham, Eugene Loring, etc., who worked equally as well staging works for films, musicals and, likewise, the ballet world. In addition, all forms of stage and screen movements from combats, water ballets, and ice

73

spectacles were requiring structured sequences of movements that elevated a variety of sports to the level of performances. A term needed to be coined that wasn't ballet specific to identify this component.

Choreography literally means "dance writing", or the connecting, structuring, or composing sequences of movement. In dressage, all of our compulsory tests are highly choreographed with very specific movements and patterns. Each is showcased to its best advantage in order that judges may determine a level of technical proficiency. These technical aspects were to be the foundation of all creative choreographic endeavors to follow.

Creating Freestyle Choreography

As with any other discipline, mastering the fundamental requirements and techniques of your level will lead to a more well-rounded and creative performance. The purpose of the Freestyle performance or any discipline's equivalent is to exhibit technical proficiency. Yes, you read that correctly - technical proficiency! Only when a horse and rider have perfected a movement to such a high degree can they perform it with maximum ease and grace. This allows the partners to express the nuances and expand the perceptions of perfection. This is the reward at the end of each level, to show how skillfully the technique is mastered so that the joy and freedom of the movement is all that is left to see.

That being said, here is a choreographic checklist to follow:

☐ **Always create a Freestyle for one level below where you are currently competing**. In order to create the most artistic Freestyle possible, it is better to have the technique fine tuned.

☐ **Know the Compulsory Movements for your level.** Review the elements in **Chapter One**.

☐ **Be Creative!** Take this opportunity to string the required movements together in new and interesting ways. Although it is understood that "test-like" choreography will cause you to lose creative points, you have to make sure that your composition is balanced. The judge does not see a copy of your choreography, so you have to ensure that it is VERY apparent to them that you have done the required compulsories on both reins without looking dull. That is easier said than done! Some judges can see the overall picture better than others.

☐ **Use the Entire Arena.** When you draw out your pattern, look at it and make sure you are not off balance or lopsided. Although the letters are great when used as markers for creating your choreography *(and practicing hitting those marks precisely will make for a more consistent performance)*, movements are not required to be executed at the letters. Play with the entire arena, using the letters as your reference point.

☐ **Always place movements in such a way that they show off your horse's strengths and mask his weaknesses.** For example, if you have a little unsettled downward transition from right lead canter to trot, plan to execute that transition in the farthest corner, away from the judge. Follow that up with something your horse does particularly well.

☐ **Remember!** You have already established your foundation in technique which is 50% of the score; now it's time to focus on the Artistic Impression which is the other 50%.

Note: Although compiling, editing, and putting together the actual music for your Freestyle may be a little overwhelming, we highly recommend that you assemble your own choreography with the help of your trainer; no one knows your horse better. You both know your horse's moods, good and bad points, and personality. Creating your own choreography will only aid in reinforcing what you already know and help you discover new things.

Where to Start

You are now ready to start your choreography. You ride your horse into the arena fully prepared to snap out a composition in one day. You turn on the music and trot around the arena expecting patterns to just flow freely. All of a sudden, you find yourself standing in the center of the arena staring blankly at the speakers and waiting for that great moment of inspiration to appear. Nothing. All of the required movements come rushing into your head at the same time, and yet nothing seems to fit together. Where do you begin?

As we mentioned in previous chapters, select your music first. Even if you don't have a completed arrangement, develop your choreography along with the music. If you have chosen a completed musical arrangement that already fits your horse's average BPMs, there already is a determined gait sequence, such as:

ENTER, HALT/SALUTE, TROT, WALK, CANTER, TROT

That's where you'll start. Listen to the music over and over again and utilize the exercises from the earlier chapters to "see" the choreography. Make a copy of the *Rules and Requirements* and the *Acceptable and Unacceptable Movements* for your level. Lay them out in front of you while you start drawing out your choreography on an arena template. Remember the exercises in **Chapter One** that asked you to time your movements in the arena? If you have timed all your compulsory movements, you are well on your way to-wards putting together your Freestyle. Draw out each of the compulsory movements in a separate arena rectangle using different color markers to indicate walk, trot, and canter. Then, indicate the movement underneath the arena box as well as your time to complete it *(see example on page 31)*. This will help you work out how long it will take to complete the required moves. The time that remains is for you to perform the moves in between. Look at your *"Acceptable Movements"* chart, and pick out the elements that you and your horse perform exceptionally well. You can showcase those in between moves in a creative way that will connect the required moves seamlessly. Don't forget your music! Now that you have determined which elements you plan on using, play around with your sheets of paper and mix up your design. Find the places in the music that best suit the composition you are creating. In the end, this method will save you a lot of time, as well as provide a record of your various performances.

Give yourself **PLENTY** of time to go through this process; it's is your chance to be creative - have fun, and try different things!

Getting Ideas for Choreography

The best place to find great ideas for innovative Freestyle compositions is by watching others. Don't confine yourself solely to watching riders at your level. Start by looking at upper level Freestyles and finding ways to modify those patterns to your level. Always keep in mind where you and your horse excel. When you are watching other rides, look for interesting points that would suit you and your horse, and write them down so you won't forget.

Step Fifteen
Building Your Choreography

 This is your instructional step-by-step "cheat sheet" for composing your Freestyle.

Items to have on hand

- ☐ Find pieces of music that fit your BPMs FIRST
- ☐ Have a copy of the *Rules and Requirements*
- ☐ Have a copy of *Acceptable/Unacceptable Rules*
- ☐ Have your timed movement journal and BPMs
- ☐ Have plenty of blank arena sheets available
- ☐ Color markers for indicating walk, trot, canter, and compulsory movement(s).

Sequence of Events:

1. Lay out your compulsory movements chart and the allowed and disallowed movement chart along with your times next to your arena template.
2. Draw out all your compulsory moves and place your times underneath each. Make sure you indicate both reins where required.
3. Select movements from the "Allowed" column that you and your horse perform well.
4. Plan your entrance and your finish first. They should both be very strong.
5. Find the musical cues within your arrangement and time them out.
6. Look for movements that compliment those cues.
7. Block out your choreography on paper so that you have something to play with the next time you ride.
8. Ride out your blocking and start discovering what works and what doesn't.
9. Map out or "score" your choreography.
10. Keep repeating this process until your patterns match the moments in the music. Don't go backwards and try and reconfigure the music to fit your ride. The more you tweak and play with the choreography and the better acquainted you become with your music, the more things will begin to gel together.

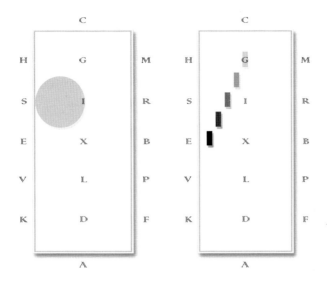

Estimated Time: 12 Sec.
Required Move:
TROT 10 Meter Circle

Estimated Time: 8 Sec.
Required Move:
TROT Leg Yield

First or Novice Level Freestyle Technical Requirements:
Maximum Time - 5:00

☐ Walk *(20m minimum continuous free walk)*

☐ 10m circle in the Trot *(both reins)*

☐ Leg Yield at the Trot *(both reins)*

☐ Lengthening stride in the Trot *(rising or sitting)*

☐ 15m circle in the Canter *(both reins)*

☐ Change of lead through the Trot *(both reins)*

☐ Lengthen stride in the Canter

79

Mapping out Your Choreography

Whenever we begin any type of performance project, be it acting, film, musical arranging, or choreography, we always create a map of the piece. In cinematic terms it's called *story-boarding*. In the case of the musical Freestyle, we start with the music and map out the story - the beginning, the middle, the end, the high points and the low points, the minor and major climaxes. Once you find those moments, you can see where the choreography has to match up. Although it's probably not the most accurate of terms, we refer to it as *"scoring"* the choreography, because we apply musical notations to the movements such as, *crescendo, ritardando, piano, forte, pace, etc.* This helps translate the music into movement so you may begin to "see" the choreography.

It is helpful to have a cue sheet that indicates when each movement change occurs. Look for specific instrumental cues within your piece of music that indicate movement change - a bell, drum, cymbal, etc. Place those cues in the third column of your chart and place the times they occurred in the first column. The middle column is reserved for the movement you will match up with those cues. If you did your timing homework earlier, you will have a good idea of what will fit in that time frame.

Sample Cue Sheet

Location in Trot Music	Movement	Musical Cue
:19	Halt/Salute	Drum
:38	Turn R into half circle	Bell
:44	Turn L into half Circle	Bell
:51	Shoulder In	Chorus

This is a useful tool to identify points within your music that will help create the most effective performance possible. Realize that this is an extremely fluid process, and that your times and movement pairings will change as you continue to refine your choreography. You will go through those changes many, many times before it feels just right. Allow yourself PLENTY OF TIME to do that. Remember, it's always much easier to modify the choreography than it is to keep changing the music.

It's Show-time
Tips and Tricks:

☐ Have your introductory music relate directly to the rest of your Freestyle. It all has to make sense.

☐ Give yourself a clear 8-count after your entry halt and salute to get yourself together. Sit tall and still.

☐ KEEP THE MUSIC GOING DURING THE HALT/SALUTE! Never, ever, ever have dead air. You will lose your audience before you even start.

☐ Do not fidget or readjust anything or "break character" during your Halt/Salute. Once you enter the arena you are "on stage", and anything that breaks that focus detracts from the performance. Adjust your pad, or whatever, **before** your music starts.

☐ SMILE - A LOT! Have fun. Once you have entered the arena, you have done all you can up to that point. Do your best performance and hope that everything follows.

☐ Let yourself get lost in the music and stay completely in the moment. Don't anticipate!

☐ Once you have committed yourself to the performance, do so 100%. No matter what happens, follow it through.

Selecting Music

Invariably, the heart of any freestyle is going to depend largely on the kinds of music you choose for your performance. In **Chapter 3: Riding with the Music - Not In Spite of It**, we wrote about the importance of making music an integral part of your riding experience. Riding "to music" instead of "with music" is akin to eating for the sake of cooking - one does not consume food to feed the desire to cook; we cook to feed our desire to eat. Likewise, we ride with music for the sake of reaching a higher level of artistic performance, companionship, and rhythmic awareness - not just for the sake of filling a sound void, or to keep our minds from thinking about the chores that are piling up back at the house. With this in mind, it's important that you choose music that is right for both you **and** your horse. Creating a freestyle based on a piece of music that you enjoy listening to in your car should **not** be your sole determining factor. Performance appeal, rhythm, musicality, and instrumentation are the key factors that should be used to determine your choices. And, of course, your partner (*that four-legged companion for whom this is all about*) should enjoy it, as well! Let's start by talking about the factors we just mentioned.

First off, let's look at what each of these key components is all about.

Performance

It's of value to note that there is a clear distinction between technical and artistic performances. It reminds me of an encounter I once had with one of my teachers at the Conservatory of Music in Puerto Rico. As part of the admission process, I had to audition in the given instrument of study - in my case, it was voice. As I stood in front of an erudite panel of instructors, I delivered my musical selection as per the guidelines set forth by the composer. When I was finished, the vocal instructor *(who would eventually become one of my dearest teachers)* looked me in the eye and said, "You performed the notes admirably, Mr. Maddlone. Now, please, let's have you sing the music." I was dumbfounded, for I thought I had done just that. In time, I would come to realize that singing the notes on a printed page was merely the beginning - just as reading these words is only the beginning of understanding.

Performance is both an artistic and technical achievement, and neither is complete without the other closely in tow. If your artistic interpretation is weak, all the technical prowess in the world will not add light and color to the performance. Likewise, a brilliant artistic performance will lose its luster if it's filled with mistakes and half-hearted passages. In freestyles, a flawless performance depends on both your technical expertise of the choreography/test chosen, and your ability to elevate the components of your chosen music beyond the mere status of background noise. As you begin to look for pieces of music to use in your freestyle, keep these points in mind:

- ☐ Does the music have an identifiable motif or cadence?

- ☐ Does the music belong to the same genre, instrumentation, or style?

- ☐ When listening to the musical selection, can you envision you and your horse riding comfortably to its beat?

- ☐ Is the music within the general range of your horse's BPMs?

By keeping these four (4) questions in mind, you can easily

eliminate musical selections that, although appealing from a listening standpoint, are not well suited as part of your intended performance. It's like the old expression goes: *It's a nice piece, but I wouldn't want to dance to it.*

Performance appeal is always a tricky and subjective issue to tackle, but one that you should keep in mind if you wish to capture the attention and imagination of your audience - and yes, the judges are part of that audience. Any good performer always considers his or her audience and it's setting before sitting down to the task of collecting musical pieces for a performance. For example, an orchestra playing at a public venue in December may dispense with marching music and opt for more traditional songs for the holiday season. Likewise, a live band playing at a dance bar will limit their slow pieces to about 30% of their repertoire in order not to drag down the overall mood of the room. When performing a musical freestyle, your audience may be varied, yet your overall thematic options are open to a wide variety of styles and moods. Additionally, the majority of folks who attend a freestyle competition are hoping to hear and see something that will raise the overall show beyond the repetitive and somewhat monotonous standards that exist when riding to a traditional test or pattern. You have a unique opportunity to elevate your routine to the level of an unforgettable performance by just paying close attention to the proper choice of music, choreography, and showmanship.

Performance Art
Webster's Dictionary Definition

Performance Art | pər ˌforməns ɑrt |
noun
"a nontraditional art form often with political or topical themes that typically features a live presentation to an audience or onlookers *(as on a street)* and draws on such arts as acting, poetry, music, dance, or painting."

In every sense of the word, a musical freestyle is nothing less than the application of music to the nuances of equestrian techniques, set within a framework of public performance for the purpose of entertainment.

Rhythm

As we saw in **Chapter Two - Rhythm and Riding**, *rhythm* is defined as *"the aspect of music comprising all the elements (as tempo, meter, and accent) that relate to forward movement"*. We then saw how tempo, meter, and accent relate to a freestyle's speed *(tempo)*, pattern *(meter)*, and phrasing *(accent)*. In a more generalized definition, *rhythm* is quite literally the beat to which everything in the world moves. Whether you are watching waves crash against the shore or your horse gallop across a pasture, each is following a set of rhythms that are inherently a part of their natural make-up. Even objects that are created for one purpose or another obey the rules of rhythm when placed in motion - windshield wipers, banners, propellers, tires, a spinning coin - each will fall into a rhythmic cadence based on its speed, pattern, and phrasing.

Although most equestrian governing bodies do not have a set definition for *rhythm* in the purest sense of the word, many do make mention of it as any set pattern of foot movements belonging to a horse *(such as the walk, trot, and canter gaits used in dressage)*. As we saw in **Chapter Two**, a horse's gait defines the very rhythm by which a horse moves within a given speed *(tempo)*, and the measurement of said speed through the use of BPMs *(**B**eats **P**er **M**inute)* gives us the means by which to incorporate music into any routine or pattern. In competition, a great deal of emphasis is placed on the use of rhythm and tempo within a performance through their appropriate use as they pertain to the varied gaits of the horse, and the high coefficients assigned as qualifiers attest to their importance.

Now, rhythm can be a tricky thing in the world of dressage.

After all, it involves two creatures *(one biped and one quad-ruped)* whose rhythmic interpretations can be easily lost in translation. Given the nature of the partnership between horse and rider, both need to listen carefully - at the music *and* each other. The horse's sense of rhythm is going to be driven by its footfalls and personality. If you've ever watched a horse ride around to a variety of styles of music, you'll quickly discover the pieces he *(or she)* likes or dislikes; a horse makes no attempt at hiding its feelings when subjected to something it doesn't like. Conversely, when a horse is riding to a piece of music whose rhythm matches their gait and mood, you'll see nothing but ears upright, bright, determined eyes, and a rounded form that moves upward into the saddle and merges with the rider.

When we addressed the matter of BPMs, we saw how horses' beats will depend on their size, confirmation, and personality. However, there are standard BPMs that apply to most horses *(see the BPM Average Table on pg. 49)*. In music, BPMs can vary wildly from one piece to another - it is one of those subjective things that are at the mercy of the composer and performer. Despite all this, most musical compositions adhere to a given tempo that identifies each with a musical style or genre. As we saw in **Chapter 3**, most pop music runs at between 115-124 BPMs, whereas dance or electronic music generally is set in the 130s, and jazz between 100 and 115.

As noted earlier, most dressage associations state that your horse does not have to adhere to a pre-determined BPM for a given gait. However, they do *(wisely)* advise that it is best to do so if you wish to present an *effective* freestyle. Of course, our goal here is to help you rise above merely being effective, and to reach that level of artistry and performance that makes your routine unforgettable. One of the best ways to achieve this is by addressing the matter of creative interpretation. And the one thing that lives at the center of creative interpretation *(in regards to dance or any moving art form)* is

86

rhythm. In the scenario where you are putting together your freestyle performance, there are three things that need to be first and foremost in your mind:

- ❖ Choreography
- ❖ Music
- ❖ Rhythm

Now, why are we stating "rhythm" here as a separate entity? After all, is rhythm not an integral part of music? The answer, of course is "yes", but rhythm - as it pertains to a freestyle - has two independent components that have to be matched: The rhythm of a chosen piece of music, and the rhythm of your horse. These two must find a common ground before you introduce them to the choreographic aspects of your ride. And - most importantly - how you decide to interpret your performance will weigh heavily on how your combined rhythms merge with your choreography. Think of it this way: Watching a plate spin on the end of someone's finger is amusing, but watching it spin while the person is on horseback is unique. It's the combination of two fairly routine yet disassociated actions that make the experience unforgettable and worthy of attention.

Tunes

If you take a quick look around you, it's pretty safe to say that you are right now within reach of some piece of technology that will play music for you, be it your computer, television, radio, MP3 player, car stereo - even your cell phone. The one thing that is prevalent in today's world is music; from advertising to entertainment, music features prominently in just about every aspect of our lives. In the equestrian world, it is no surprise that music would eventually come to play an important role in the sport. Of course, like everything else, there is a given set of musical styles and genres that best fit a given enterprise. In the world of the Kür, music depends on the rhythm and personality of two beings in order to work. But, where can you go to listen to a sampling of the plethora of styles that inundate each broadcast medium and cyberspace?

Thankfully, the Internet provides a great resource for your listening pleasure. Although there are numerous websites that offer listening stations or music samplers for you to choose from, they invariably tend to gravitate towards a given type, genre or style - be it instrumental *(heavily orchestral, 3-4 piece bands, synth-based orchestrations)* or vocal *(from full vocal segments to Karaoke samplings)*. As you begin your musical odyssey towards finding musical pieces that best fit you and your horse, it's a good idea to start big and work your way down. After all, the last thing you want to do is deny yourself a wondrous piece of music because it was whittled out on some pre-determined playlist. Here then is a quick guide to some of the places where you can start treating your ears:

Internet Radio Sites - To say the least, there are too many out there to mention in this chapter, but they are nonetheless a great starting off point for finding music that you may *(or may not)* have heard before but could not quite remember. Some of the more popular stations out there are RadioRow.com, RadioTower.com, and Live365.com. One evening, give yourself some time to enjoy a nice glass of wine or some favorite aperitifs, then sit and listen to a wide variety of musical pieces from a few of these online stations with your trusty metronome in hand. When you find something you really like, measure its BPM, and then make a note of it along with the song title, artist, and tempo. After a while, you'll have a list of music that is not only appealing, but one that suits the BPMs for your horse.

Satellite Radio - In the last few years, companies like Sirius, Worldspace and XM have placed uninterrupted musical broadcasts in the hands *(and ears)* of millions of people around the world *(as of this writing, Sirius and XM had just completed their merger, creating one of the world's largest* *satellite radio providers)*. Although terrestrial broadcasts are less expensive and more prevalent in populated cities than the subscription-based satellite services, the latter still provides a greater variety, less commercials, and access to a more eclectic variety of world music. For the musical freestyle enthusiast, satellite radio provides a wonderful musical canvas from which to explore newer, more sophisticated selections.

Online Music Stores - As with the Internet radio sites, there are a wide variety of places these days where you can go to buy music online. Basic online music purchasing sites such as iTunes, Napster, MP3.com, MusicBox *(Sony)*, JukeBox-Alive, FeedMyiPod.com, and music.yahoo.com are but a very small sampling of what is available to the digital audiophile. In the end, they all provide the means by which to purchase those song titles you've chosen to be just right for you and your horse. Once you're armed with the appropriate music selections that suit your horse's BPMs, you're well on your way towards creating an effective freestyle performance.

Standard Music Stores - If you're a purist who prefers the smell of vinyl or the feel of a nice, shrink-wrapped CD while searching for music, your neighborhood record store is a great place to start *("record store" does seem a bit nostalgic and dated here, given that the standard 33's or 45's of yesteryear have mostly been relegated to vintage shops or the "hard to find" sections of music stores)*. Most places these days have listening stations where you can enjoy either a sampling from a given album or the whole selection when making a purchase decision. In either case, be sure to bring along your metronome so you can measure the BPMs of your favorite song selections *(by the way, this is where metronome features come into play - be sure to choose a unit that has volume control and a lighted beat indicator - this way, you won't disturb the folks in nearby listening stations)*.

Public Libraries - Today, many libraries offer listening stations for folks to enjoy to vintage or rare recordings. Once again, be sure to bring along your metronome to measure out the various song selections. Call your local Public Library to find out the features they offer, plus any requirements they may have *(memberships, fees, etc)*.

Licensing

Invariably, the subject of licensing always comes up when discussing music for freestyles - and rightly so. As with any other form of creative endeavor, music is protected by copyright laws to ensure that writers/composers get remunerated for the work(s) they've created. In the United States, both **ASCAP** *(American Society of Composers, Authors, and Publishers)* and **BMI** *(Broadcast Music, Inc.)* are membership-driven organizations that watch over the rights of its members by licensing and distributing royalties for the non-dramatic public performances of their members' copyrighted works. "Licensees", as defined by these organizations, refers to any person or group who wants to perform copyrighted music publicly. Both of these associations have established alliance partnerships with other royalty accounting companies throughout the world who watch over licensing fees and royalties distributions for their members within a given country or area(s) of interest. Thus, any member of **ASCAP** or **BMI** who writes and/or publishes a piece of music may rest assured that their works are being protected worldwide.

In the United States in 2001, the **USEF** entered into a contract with both **ASCAP** and **BMI** to license all recognized and endorsed competitions and events held in the U.S. through the auspices of the **USEF**, effective July 1st of that year. Per the **USEF**, this contract provides a non-exclusive license covering all **USEF**-sanctioned competitions and exhibitions - meaning that any person riding in a recognized and endorsed show may use recorded or live music from **ASCAP** or **BMI's** repertoire in *a non-dramatic rendition.* The **USDF** further elucidates this point by noting that copyrighted music from **ASCAP** and **BMI** may be used in musical freestyles for the purpose of competition and/or entertainment purposes. Now, what are "non-dramatic renditions"? These are situations where music selections from a musical play, opera, ballet, or film score are performed separate from the given piece of work from which they came. For example: If you chose to use the song, *"Music of the Night"* from *"Phantom of the Opera"* during a riding event, that would be considered a *non-dramatic rendition*, as it is being used as part of a given venue, and not along with the rest of the score from that musical *(and thus not being performed solely for dramatic purposes)*. Another example of a *non-dramatic rendition* is when a song is used in a jukebox, broadcast over a radio station, or as part of a band's ensemble during a live performance.

Another term that is brought up is that of **mechanical *(or synchronization)* rights**. **ASCAP** and **BMI** do not license the right to record music on a CD or tape; this is something that is acquired directly from a given writer or publisher *(Harry Fox being one of the largest licensing and distribution agencies for music publishers in the United States)*. What is meant by doing a mechanical reproduction? Well, the key word in the licensing rights we just explained is to "record". For example: Let's go back to the *Phantom* analogy we used earlier. If you want to copy a segment of a recording of *"The Music of the Night"* to be used as part of your routine, you would be covered under the agreement formed under the **USEF**, as said piece of work would be part of a non-dramatic rendition. Now, if you decided to record your own version of the same song using bagpipes and kazoos *(which we would highly advise against)*, you would be required to get a licensing release from the composer and/or publisher, as you are recreating *(or reinterpreting)* the song in a way that was not originally intended by the author(s). The performing rights organizations in the United States (*ASCAP, BMI*) have over 300,000 members each, encompassing over 12 million compositions that are represented worldwide.

"Technological progress has merely provided us with more efficient means for going backwards."

Aldous Huxley

Technology

Unfortunately, this quote is quite representative in the world of the musical freestyle. Staying on top of the technological crest in music is daunting for any audiophile, and it often requires a strong and equal combination of time, money, and expertise - and most riders above the age of consent find this grouping to simply be too much to handle. So, the aim of this segment is to provide you with a crash course on the basics of technology as they pertain to your musical freestyle.

DBX, MPX, and Other Strangers

To be sure, there is no shortage of terms when it comes to audio equipment and the multitude of peripherals that surround this aural universe. It was bad enough when you had to keep track of such classics as AUX In/Out, Line In/Out, Rec Level, Mono/Stereo, or Phones. Now, thanks to the digital revolution, you have to add such niceties as CD-R, CD-R/W, MP3, MP4, Ogg, DSP, and DAW to the mix *(to name but a paltry few)*. For those of you who are "slightly" over 21, many of the terms related to music that are used today did not even exist in the vernacular of your youth. Take, for example, this popular term: Ripping and burning music. For many, they bring back memories of the days when Rock n' Roll albums were, well, quite literally ripped and burned during street rallies for the supposed "unwholesome" influence their music had on the youth of the times. Luckily, we've outgrown many of those cultural stigmas. But the nature of technical terms continues to be a perennial thorn in the side of users everywhere. So, where to begin? Well, let's start with the basics of the average playback systems, and then we'll work our way up into the many facets of record ing and reproduction.

Don't Touch That Dial

Stereo equipment has been part of the mainstream con-
sciousness since the first vacuum tube lit up and helped Re-
ginald Fessenden broadcast the first radio signal back on
December 23,1900. Since those days, radio and stereo-
phonic equipment have risen to the heights of superstardom,
and self-respecting audiophiles everywhere have been in
search of the perfect system and a "sweet" set of speakers.
By the way, don't worry about some of the terms that we'll
be blurting out in this section - **Appendix 4 - Audio Equipment Terms of Endearment** contains an explanation of the
terms we'll be referencing, along with their various interrela-
tionships. So, what do you need? Well, let's start with the
basics - your home audio entertainment system.

The Rack

For many music aficionados, this topic alone could fill a
book - luckily for you, we'll only devote a few lines. There
are two ways to go when it comes to stereo systems: The all-
in-one system that has a built-in CD player, tape deck, and
radio, or the components rack, where each individual unit is
purchased separately and hooked up to a power source for
amplification. In many instances, it all comes down to the
issues of money and functionality - how much you are will-
ing to spend, and how functional will a modular system be
for you and your needs. If you happen to have a large collection of records, tapes, and CDs, and you've always
wanted to transfer some of your collection to CD or MP3s,
then it would behoove you to invest in a modular system,
and purchase those items *(CD player/recorder, turntable,
dual tape deck, etc.)* that would best suit your needs. Oth-
erwise, one of the more upscale entertainment systems *(or
"bookshelf" stereos)* would be sufficient to handle all your
listening & recording needs.

If you're looking to get a unit that you can use both in the house and out in an arena, we suggest you look at the wide variety of portable stereos *(or "boom boxes", as they are commonly referred to)* that are out on the market today. If you choose to go with this, make sure that,

- ❑ It can be operated with electricity or batteries,
- ❑ It has a remote control for tape/CD operation and volume control,
- ❑ The power output per channel is greater than 35 watts,
- ❑ The speakers can be detached for better placement,
- ❑ The unit contains "Line In" and "Line Out" ports for connecting to/from peripherals,
- ❑ The unit can transfer *(dub)* the contents of a CD onto a cassette,
- ❑ The CD player can handle regular *("store bought")* CD's, CD-R's *(MP3 or WMA encoded CDs)*, and CD-R/W's,
- ❑ The CD player has a skip protection setting to keep the soundtrack from skipping if the unit is moved during playback.

There are many portable stereo units out there that are fairly compact and easy to transport, while others tend to be a bit heavier and more imposing to the eye. Remember: You're going for functionality here; don't be persuaded to buy a unit because it looks like it came from a NASA garage sale. Keep the features mentioned above in mind, and you should find something that will serve you well both in and out of the arena.

Now, if you choose to go the modular route, let's explore some of the main components that should be a "must have" in your equipment collection.

Tape Decks

Although CDs are rapidly becoming the de facto source for

music in freestyle dressage competitions, many places still insist on using cassette tapes as back-ups. Indeed, many associations still contain verbiage in their manuals stating that CDs **and** tapes are requested for both the main and back-up units during competition.

That being said, you want to look for a deck that can do a wide variety of things, both in playback and recording mode. If possible, find a tape deck that has servomechanisms on both capstans for playback and rewind - this helps to keep the surface tension on the tape even, and will ensure you don't run into the tape eating problems that normally occur when a tape gets wrapped around the spindles due to uneven rewinding speeds. Noise reduction is always a plus when you have a tape deck - look for unit that supports Dolby B & C. With today's ubiquitous access to digital music, noise reduction is no longer a "must have" for home use beyond the tape deck, as the signal-to-noise ratio used for recording on CDs and creating MP3's is pretty high. Another thing to look for is a digital counter - when editing tapes, a digital counter will be more accurate for marking sections on your tape. If possible, look for a tape deck that contains a sensor for finding the beginning or end of a song *(the unit does this by noting the "dead areas" on the tape surface where nothing is recorded)* - when searching for a given selection, this feature helps to speed up the process. Finally, a dual deck unit comes in handy if you're looking to dub tapes for performance. Since you're required to bring along two (2) copies of your music to a competition, a dual deck will allow you to create a copy in no time.

CD Players

Since CDs have become such a part of the musical landscape, this medium will most probably be the one you'll come to rely on when preparing for a freestyle competition. Given that most of today's computers can burn music CDs from MP3 or WAV-encoded files, you want to make sure that your CD player can handle those formats. Many of the older players can only read the "store bought" variety, and will flash a "NO DISC" sign when you insert a CD that you've burned on your Mac or PC. So, here are some of the main items you should keep in mind when purchasing a CD player:

☐ Must read regular *("store bought")* CDs, CD-R's *(MP3 or WMA encoded CDs)*, and CD-R/W's,

☐ Should have a reliable tracking motor *(with a sizable anti-skip buffer)* for guiding the laser beam that reads the **CD** *(if it's a portable unit, then this is a "must have" feature)*,

☐ Has a "Line Out" for both digital and analog signals, so you may transfer the music onto an analog tape deck or a digital tape *(DAT)*,

☐ Has a remote control,

☐ Has a headphone jack with separate volume control

There are a wide variety of features that come with CD players, to include automatic ejection panels, touch-sensitive controls, bass/treble enhancement settings, control lock-down switches, etc. Although these are nice options to have, make sure that the basics noted above are there before you chance to buy a unit. In the end, we're looking for a deck *(or portable unit)* that will make your freestyle performance practice and preparation that much easier and enjoyable.

Turntables

OK, it may seem like we're going a bit "retro" here but, in truth, a good turntable may just be what you need to find some of those lost musical treasures locked away in your closet or attic. As much as we like to search for music that is fresh and appealing to a wider audience, there are some old traditional "classics" out there that may suit you and your horse to a tee. The challenge you're going to have is in transferring songs from vinyl to a digital medium so you can effectuate a selection's BPM, or chop it up accordingly to match a given time segment or passage.

There are two ways to go here - traditional turntables or **USB** models. There is a third option - the laser turntable - but the cost of such a unit far outweighs its merits for our basic equipment scenario. If you already have a turntable, then you probably have it connected to your modular stereo system. Check to make sure that you can dub directly from the turntable to a tape *(or DAT)* source; that will allow you to transfer the music over for editing. If you have one of the newer USB turntables, then you are already set-up to sample music directly from your old vinyl records into your computer.

If you haven't purchased a turntable yet *(or never had a need until your Aunt Sally gave you her collection of Benny Goodman records)*, here are some tips to look for when going out to get a platter:

1. Be sure the unit has a direct drive motor. Although many of the newer models have this as standard equipment, there are some out there that are still belt-driven,

2. Make sure the tone arm has adjustable counter-weights and anti-skating adjustments,

3. The unit should have a dust cover,

4. Make sure you get a quality stylus

Because of the waning popularity of vinyl records, turntables are finding a niche more so amongst performance musicians, who use the platters for various scratching effects *("turn-tablism")*, where the music on the record itself is secondary to the sounds that emanate from the platter when it is moved back and forth in a rhythmic pattern. This performance style has increased the popularity of turntables amongst the newer generation of musicians/performers, though the availability of quality turntables still remains scarce.

Speakers

If we were to equate a stereo system to the human body, then the speakers would surely be the voice. And there's nothing that will lessen the enjoyment of a good musical piece more than a substandard set of speakers or head-phones. Since we are dealing here with equipment that will best serve your freestyle performance objectives, we're going to confine our comments to speakers that can be used in the more inhospitable environment of the indoor/outdoor arena.

As you begin to expose your horse to the wonders of music, you will invariably notice his or her reticence when ap-proaching the speakers for the first time. Usually, it's be-cause of the sound they make and the volume at which they're set. Sometimes it's merely because they do not find a given set of frequencies to their liking. Horses, by nature, have a superb auditory sense, and thus their sensitivity to loud or unpleasant noises is something you must keep in mind at all times *(in some studies, horses have been known to hear a sound from as far as 2.75 miles away, or 4,400 me-ters)*. Therefore, when choosing a set of speakers, you want to ensure that the signal range they cover is fairly wide, that they will not create crackling or popping sounds when the volume is turned very low, and that the quality or gauge of speaker wire used is appropriate for the placement of the speakers in relation to the music source. Here are some guidelines to follow:

1. Since the average human can pick up sounds from

20Hz to 20kHz, and a horse's range goes *(on average)* from 55Hz to 33.5kHz, you want to get speakers/headphones that can at least handle a frequency response between 20Hz and 20kHz.

2. Whenever possible, get three-way speakers - they are better equipped to faithfully recreate the high's and low's of the sound spectrum.

3. Make sure that your speakers are resistant to dust, temperature changes, and moisture. Some manufacturers like Bose, Cerwin Vega, Infinity, and AR *(Acoustic Research)* offer some great outdoor models that would fare well under most inclement conditions.

Speaker wire is of great importance when you want to get the optimal sound from your speakers. General rule of thumb:

**The thicker the wire, the better it can pass
an amplified audio signal.**

The thickness is rated by its **AWG** *(American Wire Gauge)* classification; the lower the number, the better the throughput. Distance is also a factor - the longer the distance from the receiver, the thicker the wire has to be in order to effectively pass the signal with little degradation in the sound. Here's a quick reference guide you can use:

Distance from speaker to stereo unit	Gauge
Under 80 feet	16
80 to 200 feet	14
Over 200 feet	12

When measuring for the required length, run a string along the path the speaker wire will follow, taking into considera-

99

tion every bend, corner, and surface indentation the wire will have to travel, as this will affect the sound quality if you don't measure accurately.

Catch a WAV

Back in the olden days *(i.e. circa 1980)*, the way to edit music beyond the confines of a professional recording studio was to mix and match edit points on a standard cassette or reel-to-reel tape deck. With the advent of the personal computer, a new means of editing became accessible in the form of audio editing software. The first iterations of these software were complex and expensive, and were geared primarily towards the professional studio musician or sound engineer. Eventually, manufacturers such as Sonic Foundry saw the potential for a simplified version of these programs and, within a few short years, the market was flooded with programs geared towards Windows and Apple users, with parameters that ranged from simple to supremely complex.

Today, there are a plethora of programs out there that will allow you to edit, mix, and burn your own songs in a manner of minutes. As with most applications, each contains features that appeal to everyone from the budding musician to the stay-at-home audiophile. Question is: What do you need in order to prepare a musical selection for your freestyle? Well, let's look at the kinds of programs that are out there, then briefly discuss those parameters that will mean the most to you in the arena.

Get Me My Editor!

In order to make this simple, let's look at the two main types of music programs that will be of most use to you: **Audio Editing Software** and **Digital Audio Workstations** *(DAWs)*. An *Audio Editing software* is simply that - a program that allows you to edit the audio files you need to mix together for your freestyle. In contrast, *Digital Audio Workstations (or **DAWs**)* allow you take those edited audio files and put them to-

100

gether, effect them, add instruments if necessary, and bounce them down into a stereo music file for playback. Huh? OK - Let's go down one level further.

When a computer "hears" a piece of music, it needs to translate that into its own digital language *(those lovely "1's" and "0's" we often hear about)* in order to manipulate the file per your instructions. In order to keep us humans from having to read endless streams of numbers, these digital files are visually represented for us in the form of sound waves on the screen. At first glance, they appear to be a quirky, horizontal version of a Rorschach test but, in reality, they are simple, graphical representations of the musical high's and low's performed within that given snippet of sound.

An Audio Editing program reads those wave files in, then gives you the necessary tools to change that piece of music into what you need for your given project. For example: You can,

- ❏ Change the speed *(tempo)* at which the music plays,
- ❏ Add special effects such as reverb, or even reverse the direction of the playback,
- ❏ Cut the wave into pieces, thus selecting only the parts you wish to use,
- ❏ Take away unwanted ambient noise, like the pops and clicks you hear on old vinyl recordings,
- ❏ Add your voice recording to a file,
- ❏ Convert the music file into a different format, such as MP3, Ogg Vorbis, or AIFF

Of course, these features we just mentioned are but the tip of the iceberg, but you get the general idea - audio editors *change* a sound file into a variant of its former self.

A **DAW**, on the other hand, takes over where the audio editor ends. Digital Audio Workstations allow you to incorporate a series of wave files into a special arrangement window, thus giving you the capability of building a song file using your edited files. Although most DAWs contain a built-in audio editor, some are not as feature-laden as the stand-alone editing programs. DAWs also allow you to add vocals, instruments either through live recordings or the use of MIDI-based keyboards/synthesizers, special sound effects, and a host of other features. Unlike the audio editing programs, many of the DAWs out there can be complex in nature, as they assume you to have some cursory experience in manipulating sound files. If you've never experimented with editing sound files before, the learning curve on a DAW can be daunting. Thankfully, there are several programs out there that make the experience not only palatable, but fun to use. In order to help you choose a set of programs that will fit your needs, we've included a table in **Appendix 5** that shows you the top 5 audio editing and DAW programs out there, along with features that are essential to your music editing needs.

As with any investment you make towards the creation of your freestyle, you need to approach this aspect of the process with a bit of quiet introspection. Although there is a great deal of personal satisfaction in creating your routine from scratch, there are many pitfalls you'll encounter that, in the long run, will cost you more than a few dollars and some hours of your time. In the realm of the musical freestyle, there are key elements that directly affect the success or failure of your performance - coaching, training, practice, choreography, the right tack, and the right music. Each involves a partnership with one or more people in order to bring out the best you and your horse have to offer in the arena at the moment of performance. Taking unnecessary shortcuts in any of these areas will further increase your level of difficulty when attempting to achieve the ultimate level of presentation and professionalism, and you owe it to yourself, your horse, and your trainer not to create these unwanted obstacles. In the end, how you value your time *(and that of your horse)* will be the key to your ultimate success. Allow yourself every opportunity to get involved in each aspect of your freestyle - the more you know about your music and choreography, the better prepared you'll be both mentally and artistically. However, when it comes to developing and preparing each of these components, be sure to rely on the expertise and training of your support group. In the end, you'll be using everyone's time and training to their best advantage.

Preparing for a Show

Probably the single most frustrating thing that can happen to you in the life cycle of your freestyle performance has nothing to do with its development, but rather in its broadcast. We have witnessed top riders disqualified because, at the moment of truth, their tape or CD would not play due to faulty mastering, or onsite equipment that was unable to handle the format(s) chosen during the final mix. After having worked so hard and spent untold months or even years to reach the level of freestyle performance, the last thing you want to hear coming from the speakers in the arena is silence.

Although most organizing bodies are specific in requesting audiocassette tapes and/or CDs from their competitors, little or nothing is documented in regards to the types of tapes and CDs that may be used. Additionally, there are no guidelines set forth indicating the type of audio equipment each venue should have on hand to ensure that all types of formatted tapes and CDs play without any interruptions.

So how do you prepare for a performance whose equipment requirements will vary from place to place? Well, until such time when the requirements are standardized, you will need to appeal to the technology's most common denominators. Here are some guidelines to follow:

Audiocassettes: Try using a chrome-based tape, as these tend to have a better than average sound reproduction than those tapes marked "normal bias". To protect your final tape mix, be sure to either remove or cover the write-protection tab on the top of the cassette *(see the label instructions in the inside of the cassette case)*.

CDs: When burning CDs at home *(or through a professional recording studio)*, make sure that only CD-R type disks are used - avoid using CD-R/W types! The "R" on the CD-R disks stands for "Read Only"; once you burn the information onto these types of disks, you cannot erase or write over the data. These types of CDs first hit the market in the late '80's when computer CD burners came onto the scene, so they enjoy a greater support infrastructure amongst home-based music CD players. CD-R/W disks are "Read/Write" enabled, meaning that you can reuse them by erasing or writing over the data stored on the disk. Since this type of CD was designed primarily for data storage, not all music CD players out there are capable of reading their header records, and thus the player will treat it as an unreadable disk.

Players: Bring along your own! These days, you can find a wide variety of portable tape and CD players that are easy to use, and whose format standards cover a wide array of tape/CD types. If you decide to go this route, be aware that the venue may not be able to plug your unit into their existing stereo system - and, more often than not, the person earmarked to operate the system will not know much of its operation beyond the basic plug and play. There is a way to get around this:

Bring along your own cabling. This is much less complicated than it sounds. Of course, it is all contingent on the type of portable unit you have. If possible, make sure your tape and/or CD unit has a "Line Out" jack in the back where you can plug in either a set of left/right RCA cables, or a standard ¼ stereo plug *(the kind you normally see on the end of your standard headphone cables)*. If the venue has a stereo system with an "AUX IN" jack, you can simply plug your unit there, then have them switch the output from "TAPE/CD" to "AUX" - your unit will then play through their speaker system.

If this scenario does not exist *(or you find yourself lacking the right kind of cabling),* bring along a portable set of powered speakers *(most boom boxes have these built-in)* and plug them into your unit *(most probably using the standard ¼ stereo plug we discussed earlier - you can find portable (battery) powered speakers at small electronics stores like Radio Shack).* You can then hold the announcer's microphone up to the speakers to broadcast your music. It may not produce the highest quality sound, but it will keep you from getting disqualified due to a lack of music.

Remember: all associations encourage you to test your music with the local venue before the show starts - some even will allow one (1) member of your party to be present in the broadcasting booth during the playback to assist with any problems that may arise with your CD or tape. Take advantage of these opportunities, and do what you can to ensure your music will be heard!

"They say Princes learn no art truly, but the art of horsemanship. The reason is, the brave beast is no flatterer. He will throw a prince as soon as his groom."
Ben Johnson

Dr. Volker Moritz

Dr. Volker Moritz

Dr. Moritz has been actively riding and training horses for over 45 years, from training level to Grand Prix. During his tenure as a rider, he has won numerous top seated dressage events through Grand Prix, and was awarded the German Federation's Golden Riders' Badge. Dr. Volker trained under such equestrian luminaries as Herbert Behrendt, General Horst Niemack, Robert Scmidtke, and Fritz Tempelmann, and credits them as the people who most influenced his education as a dressage rider.

Dr. Moritz's career as a judge has spanned over 37 years, receiving his classification as an internationally recognized FEI "O" judge in 1980. He has presided over many national and international championships for seniors and young riders in Europe and North America. He's been an active member of the ground jury at such prestigious events such as the 1998 World Equestrian Games in Rome, the 2000 Olympic Games in Sydney, and the 2002 World Equestrian Games in Jerez, to name but a few. He has also served as an active jury member at the CDIO event in Aachen, Germany every year since 1972, and as President since 2001. Dr. Moritz is also one of six (6) judges who were selected by the FEI to assess and direct the courseware for the FEI Judge program.

EquiChord is honored and proud to include Dr. Volker's thoughts on freestyles and dressage in this book. We hope that they will be an inspiration to our readers, as they have been for us and countless of his students throughout the world.

An Interview with Dr. Volker Moritz

What do you think is the biggest misconception concerning dressage?

Many riders do not understand the concept of the horse as an athlete. When people ask me what sport I'm in, and I reply that I'm a dressage rider, they look at me and say, "oh, that's easy - you're sitting down all the time!" Yet, what they do not realize is that, from a physical aspect, a dressage rider requires more strength and stamina than a show jumper. It is much harder work from a physical standpoint to ride correct dressage. Now, in speaking of the way to reach your goal as a top seated rider, you must aspire to achieve lightness and harmony in both your riding and the relationship with your horse. A happy and submissive horse, trained in every sense as an athlete, will only achieve his or her full potential if the rider approaches his or her training in a likewise fashion.

In regards to training - what do you think is the most common problem people run into when developing a training program?

Many people do not understand that it takes 4 to 5 years to educate a horse to Grand Prix level - and that's assuming the horse has the talent to reach such a level; this is yet another issue that many people do not understand. Some believe that, because a horse carries an expensive price tag, it will have the talent to do Grand Prix. This could not be farther from the truth. Additionally, the mindset of the rider/trainer is key to the proper development of a horse beyond the issue of mere physical strength. Technique is one of the fundamental keys to training, as is experience. As a rider/trainer, you need to know how to call upon past experiences to overcome a given problem with a horse; how to apply a solution today based on a problem that happened to a similar horse three years before. So many people do not understand this concept.

So you see dressage training as a long-term process?

Yes, to be sure. When you start riding when you are ten or fifteen years old, it is fine - you have more elasticity, more endurance, and a better ability to feel the horse's movements and how to swing with him. You can set very specific goals for yourself to reach a certain level of perfection when you're young; its much harder to achieve those same goals when you start later in life. When you start any sport later on in life, you must accept the limitations that come with that tardiness, and simply enjoy it and have fun. Just because you buy a tennis racket or a bicycle doesn't mean that you can aspire to be a Roger Federer or Lance Armstrong in just a few weeks or months - that takes time and training.

As a judge, what are some of the inherent problems or obstacles you see concerning freestyles today?

Well, I have been judging for 40 years now, and have judged freestyles in international, PSG, CDI-1, and Grand Prix competitions - all upper levels. I have seen some wonderful performances, and some awful ones as well. In 90% of the cases, the music is too loud; I have seen horses literally run away with the riders when the music started to play. Horses are very sensitive to sounds, and they frighten easily when the music is too loud. The second thing that always concerns me is the harmonic choices riders make. I tend to be very tolerant with young people when they ride pony freestyles, for example. They want to have happier music and try new things, and I understand that. But sometimes music can become too caustic if not properly mixed or transitioned, and I can only be tolerant up to a point. Regardless of the age group, music needs to fit the horse, and be a proper fit for both the horse and rider; it must show the horsemanship and proficiency of both. Unfortunately, you sometimes can clearly see that the music does not fit at all; there is no correlation between the beat, the rider, and the horse.

109

Do you think that basic training in freestyles needs to reach a wider audience amongst equestrian enthusiasts?

Yes, I do. In some of the larger venues in Europe, there is a fellow who does a lot of music for many international riders. Once, during one of his clinics, he played some music during a freestyle demonstration, and asked the audience if the music fit the horse's trot. When the audience responded "no", he played the music a little faster and then a little slower, each time asking the audience if it fit with the horse's foot falls. Eventually, he hit upon the right tempo, and the audience immediately responded positively. In about 10 minutes, he was instructing the audience as to which piece of music fit a given gait on the horse. Once the audience knew the difference in the beats per minute, he easily demonstrated how a simple adjustment in speed could make the music fit an extended canter, a walk, and so on.

We know that, as a judge, you cannot show any partiality amongst the active riders. But, what is your opinion on the manner in which competitors today prepare for a freestyle competition?

Well, I was part of the freestyle forum in Ankun Germany; it was the first time that we had had a freestyle forum of this size, so there were many riders, trainers, and spectators on hand. Anky Van Grunsven's composer was on hand to give a demonstration. It was amazing to see how he developed the music, and how long the entire process took. First, they have a meeting where they discuss the process, pointing out where the music needs to be a bit more interesting, more inspiring, and so on. Every movement, every foot fall is studied to make sure that each is represented by the music correctly. This could take up to 2 to 3 months to get ready. Then she rehearses it upwards of 200 times before she steps into a competitive arena. But she understands the work that it requires, and knows how to put it all together. As I said before, the process towards excellence does not happen overnight.

Chapter Five
The FEI and Upper Levels Revealed

"When I bestride him, I soar, I am a hawk: he trots the air; the earth sings when he touches it; the basest horn of his hoof is more musical than the pipe of Hermes."
William Shakespeare, Henry V

HISTORY

Dressage today is an amalgam of both recent and ancient histories. Its roots sprung from military maneuvers crafted centuries ago. Although Xenophon's work has been cited as the oldest known work on horsemanship in the Western world, Kikkuli in the East wrote a text in Hittite around 1400 BC that carefully outlined the conditioning of the horse. As a master equestrian and charioteer, he detailed in his writings all aspects of proper balanced conditioning, including the recommended use of interval training astride before introducing a horse to chariot work. His methods of conditioning and training are uncannily similar to the regimen used by Eventers today.

Each and every movement we perform has its beginnings in these and similar teachings. Our development as a species was heavily reliant on our relationship with the horse, and is one of the few universal constants, as is our appreciation of rhythm and music. Even in those military expeditions from long ago, drum rhythms were used in parades to maintain uniformity among the legions. Rhythm, and in some forms, music, have always joined forces organically with the horse.

They are creatures of rhythm whose innate beat lends itself to all forms of musical expression.

The extended history of the horse's relationship with music is sketchy at best. Since horses have been such an integral and revered part of the development of man, it is hard to imagine them not being part of the ancient musical spectacles of Egypt, Greece, and Rome, to name but a few. In humanity's more recent history, the introduction of the indoor arena during the Renaissance and the formation of Federico Grisone's riding academy in Naples in 1532, is most likely what gave rise to ongoing exhibitions of military maneuvers on horseback, and the beginnings of modern dressage. These fledgling performances were most likely accompanied by live music. It wasn't until the establishment of the Spanish Riding School in Vienna, Austria in 1572, that Haute Ecole movements and military maneuvers were specifically choreographed, set to music, and performed for the exclusive enjoyment of the court and its guests.

The period from the Baroque through the beginning of the 1900s produced a wealth of written materials regarding the technique and theory behind the development of horse and rider. Numerous books and treatise were written by such equestrian luminaries as François Robichon de la Guerinier, Eisenberg, Andrade, and Marialva. Prestigious riding schools such as the Cadre Noire in Saumur, France were established based on the principles set forth in these works.

Rebirth of The Olympics

The modern day Olympic games were revived in Athens, Greece on April 6, 1896, with 14 countries participating. Equestrian jumping was introduced in 1900 in Paris, as part of the Exposition Universelle Internationale - the Paris World's Fair.

In 1912 at the Olympic Games in Stockholm, Sweden, dressage was introduced as part of the military competition. It was a segment of combined training that included cross country maneuvers and jumping - not unlike our Eventers of today. From then on, equestrian events began to blossom as spectator activities. With this new venue available, along with the changing times and the shift of economies, the Spanish Riding School opened up its coveted performances to the general public in 1918 in order to continue to maintain the school.

It wasn't until 1950 that civilians were actually permitted to compete in Eventing and, before then, only a handful of civilian riders had competed in the other equestrian disciplines. Women were allowed to compete in dressage in 1952, making it one of the few sports today were men and women compete on an equal basis. Up until that point, only members of the military had easy access to a high level of classical training. With armies evolving to more advanced technologies, cavalries were phased out, and other venues had to be created in order to keep the equestrian arts alive. Many members of the military went on to establish civilian careers around the world as trainers, riders, judges, and breeders.

The heavy military influence within the sport produced a very strict perspective and delineation between the discipline of basic maneuvers and the evolution of these movements into spectator friendly events. These older values were heavily instilled upon each rider in an attempt to maintain the purity of the sport. It is out of this concern and reticence that Freestyles have, in some circles, been viewed as a major detractor of good technique.

Competitive Freestyles did not make the scene until much later in its history. The first **Kür** *(or musical Freestyle)* performed at an international level was in 1979 in Goodwood, England. It wasn't until 1996 in Atlanta, Georgia that Freestyles were brought into the Olympic Games. This first Olympic venue for Freestyles became the highest attended equestrian event at the games. Since the introduction of Freestyles into competition, dressage itself has become the fastest growing equestrian pursuit.

Freestyles Today

Major Competitions

There are many levels of competition that are organized and sanctioned by the FEI ranging from Pony and Children's divisions, to Junior and Young Rider divisions. In addition to the major events, CDI *(Concours de Dressage International)*, competitions are organized by region or league to qualify various riding levels for competitions.

The venues that get the most media attention and can sometimes be seen on television are:

- The Olympics
- The World Cup
- The Pan American Games
- The European Championships

For more information on FEI competitions and their schedules, please visit the FEI website, or contact the FEI at:

www.fei.org

International Freestyle Stars

It is hard to talk about the growth of Freestyles without making mention of the star horses and riders that have built up the sport's popularity along the way. Instead of focusing on just the top winning riders on the technical side, we decided to highlight the top performances from a musical and artistic perspective. Thanks to venues like YouTube and others, these magnificent performances are being shared with a worldwide audience, and have become some of the most important vehicles that Freestyles have today. We decided to democratically select, not only the Freestyles that we felt most excelled in their class, but also the most viewed on the Internet as a part of our "Best Of" list. They are compiled in order of appearance, and in the order of importance we believe they have generated towards the advancement of the artistic, musical, and performance aspects of the sport - as well as their popularity on the web *(as of this book's publication)*.

Dr. Reiner Klimke - Ahlerich - Madison Square Garden 1987 - 51,839 viewed on one entry

In this early exhibition, the great master, Dr. Klimke, gave us a glimpse into what equine dancing partners can really aspire to be. He used contemporary 80's music along with a Beatles tribute to put together a fun, audience-rousing routine that could stand up against some of today's best. It is always remarkable to observe someone who had such a magnificent mastery of the technique along with a keen understanding of showmanship. The perfected technique and the talent of horse and rider gave this pair the freedom to completely release and create the illusion that every movement was effortless and spontaneous. The audience can sit back and enjoy the performance because these performers had complete command of every nuance of their routine. What wonderful Freestyles would Dr. Klimke have shown us today?

Dr. Reiner Klimke - Ahlerich and Anna-Grethe Jensen - Marzog Pas De Deux

Barbara Strawson, a friend and an accomplished FEI Grand Prix rider/trainer, recently shared this video with us of a Freestyle exhibition ride done in the mid 1980s. Although Freestyles as a "legitimate" aspect of competition were still in their infancy and not yet recognized as an Olympic event, Dr. Klimke and Ms. Jensen displayed not only their command of the technique, but their innate showmanship. The

115

routine is spellbinding, and the entrance use of Khatcha-turian's music precisely compliments and showcases this classic performance. We highly recommend that this rendition be seen by anyone pursuing Freestyles for pleasure or performance.

Anky van Grunsven - Bonfire - Sydney Olympics 2000 - 104,214 views from one entry

This Freestyle is the one that showed the possibility of things to come. The music was designed for Anky by Alie Schoenberg from an orchestral arrangement of Neil Diamond's music. Even though you may not be a big fan of this type of orchestration, the brilliance of this performance is in the time, effort, and precision with which it was constructed. In a published interview with Alie Schoenberg, he commented on the ongoing choreographic collaboration he had with Anky and her trainer/ husband, Sjeff Janssen. They carefully worked out the choreography to flow organically along with the music's highs and lows. Alie and Anky worked on this with the same dedication as any professional performer would when preparing for a show. He also shared that she knew every beat of the music, and had practiced it at least 200 times to get the nuances and the feeling just right. That is why she excels in this element of the sport, because she takes it extremely seriously and approaches every aspect with the dedication of a true artist.

There is no question that Anky continues to set the standard for Freestyles. Her dynamic performances are crafted with a dedication and understanding that has yet to be equaled. It is her method and approach that should be studied as the foundation from which to grow.

Andreas Helgstrand - Blue Hors Matine - WEG 2006 - 7,337,333 views on one entry

Blue Hors Matine has become somewhat of a superstar from this video. The energy and enthusiasm of this pair, along

116

with the fun and accessibility of the music, made this performance a milestone in the sport. The highlight of this Freestyle is the incredible ending Passage and Piaffe sequence performed by this talented mare in perfect syncopation to *Lady Marmalade*. Andreas made the bold choice to perform with contemporary music as opposed to the safer, inexpressive classical orchestral renditions or techno selections that seem to have been more commonly preferred by the judges. Granted, he was riding a mare that many would consider to be the Sylvie Guillem of the horse world. Nevertheless, the joy and showmanship they both displayed had the audience on their feet by the final Halt/Salute. This single performance has brought in an amazing number of online viewers from riders and non-riders alike with over seven million hits. That is an incredible number for any one video, and a vivid testament to the magic this performance generates.

Anky Van Grunsven - Keltec Salinero - WEG2006 - 819,657 views on one entry

With yet another horse, Anky continues to repeat her Freestyle success through her careful choreography and the well-constructed music. Anky enjoys bringing out the subtleties and elegance of her rides, rather than relying solely on dramatic punctuation. She is one of the few riders who ends her routines with a beautiful, soft statement. It is highly effective and memorable without being anti-climatic. Some may argue that the Edith Piaf retrospective may not have been the most popular musical choice in and of itself. However, given that a good overall performance is made from the sum of its parts, this routine holds together brilliantly. In March of 2008, Anky won her unprecedented ninth FEI World Cup.

Edward Gal - Gestion Lingh - WEG2006 - 55,322 views on one entry

Edward Gal was Anky van Grunsven's student at the time of this competition, and it is very apparent in this Freestyle that

117

her influence and talent were generously imparted to her pupil. The music is a techno reworking of several strong, dramatic and emotional orchestral pieces, such as Samuel Barber's *Adagio for Strings*. This is, and has always been, one of our personal favorites. As such, we would like to do a bit of analysis on the high points of this performance, and what we see as its major accomplishments.

One of the most challenging aspects of compiling a Grand Prix Freestyle is the seamless flow of music between the Passage and Piaffe sequences into the trot and the extended trot. Since there is such a huge disparity in the BPMs, this is where most arrangements will suffer from that "radio dial effect" we wrote about earlier. Since a higher degree of difficulty is rewarded for the frequent changes between these gaits, it can be quite challenging to create a supportive score that doesn't sound odd or disjointed. In Edward's freestyle, he enters with a contemporary arrangement of chants that are heavily underlined with a fabulous percussion section that supports the first passage and piaffe. As in most of the more appealingly compiled Freestyles, the music appropriately underscores everything, even the Halt/Salute at the beginning. The music and percussion build to a chilling yet lyrical release into the trot, supported by a very powerful and contemporary arrangement of Samuel Barber's *Adagio for Strings*. His half pass sequence builds again to a release into the extended trot across the diagonal. What makes this portion of the performance so wonderful is the dimension sustained by the juxtaposition of the mournful melody on top of the expressive and driving percussion section. The intimacy with which Edward relates to his music is most apparent when he carefully half halts Lingh in the corner as they build momentum for the peak accent, as the first strike of the extended trot hits the downbeat of the music. The weakest point of the music is the transition into the walk, due to the music selected. It is the only portion that doesn't seem to fit as cohesively as the rest. The music comes in too abruptly and seems to stylistically fit more with Anky's Freestyle than

118

this one. This drastic change pulls the spectator out of the mood that had been so carefully created up to that point.

The transition into the canter does regain the theme and leads the audience back into the moment. The strong and dynamic canter portion ebbs and flows into and out of the pirouettes, underscored by a lilting call to Allah. Once again, although there is a strong and energetic percussive line enhancing the power of the horse, there is also a beautiful, lyrical melody and a violin line layered on top that bring out the lightness and elegance of the pair along with the drama.

Dr. Cesar Parra - Galant Du Serein - Devon 2006 - 20,243 views on one entry

This particular video is a tribute for Galant who passed away in 2007. The Freestyle was originally done to an arrangement highlighted by the music of Shakira. Dr. Parra is one of today's dressage luminaries who has a strong passion for the advancement of the sport - particularly Freestyles. His guidance and insights on international competition and the realities of preparing Freestyles at the upper levels have been invaluable. We can only wait with great anticipation to see the musical wonders that are yet to come.

FEI Demystified

The progression up the **FEI** ladder is the goal of every horse/ rider involved in international competition. Since one of the primary functions of the **FEI** is to oversee equestrian development leading to the Olympic games, the focus of most continental and world competitions are to develop athletes who can compete at the highest levels. These qualifications consist of the successful mastery of the Grand Prix, Grand Prix Special, and Grand Prix Freestyle *(Kür)* tests.

Based on the results of the Grand Prix test at individual competitions, teams are given medals and individuals are qualified for the Grand Prix Special. Only the top horse/ rider combinations can progress to that level. From there, only the best of the best horse/riders, based on total points from the previous two tests, will qualify for the final medal round - the Grand Prix Freestyle *(Kür)* test.

Qualifying

Each major event has it's own set of qualifying parameters. To start with, the competitive areas are broken up into Regions or Leagues. For example, Western Europe, Eastern Europe, North America, South America, etc. The geographical regions may change depending on the category. For example, the World Cup Dressage for Young Riders competitions are broken up into 5 Regions/Leagues; whereas the Olympic qualifying system breaks the groups into 7 geographical regions.

Here is an example. You are a winning Grand Prix rider and you want to take your horse to the Olympics. Your goal will be to achieve the minimum standard requirements to participate. In the case of the Olympics, a minimum score of 64% must be given to the horse/rider combination from two different FEI Official International Dressage Judges of a nationality other than that of the rider. In addition, that score must be achieved at two different sanctioned and recognized CDI competitions.

Qualifying for the World Cup finals is tied very closely to succeeding in the Grand Prix Freestyle. In order to qualify for the World Cup, the horse/rider are required to complete at least three Musical Freestyles at a CDI-W. From there, an overall score is determined by taking an average of the three qualifying musical rides. Therefore, the final classification is determined by placement in the Grand Prix Freestyle.

Once again, it is extremely important that the rider verify their own qualifying requirements for each show. Every event can be different and the rules are constantly being amended. Therefore, frequently double-checking your Region's or League's rules is highly recommended.

The FEI Freestyle Tests and Competition

There are only five (5) recognized **FEI** Freestyle tests available for international competition. They are as follows:

- ❖ **Pony Riders**
- ❖ **Juniors**
- ❖ **Young Riders**
- ❖ **Intermediare 1**
- ❖ **Grand Prix**

Rules and Requirements

Pony Rider Freestyle Test*
Rider Eligibility

 Children between the ages of 12-14 years old who have won qualifying competitions within their regions.

FEI Pony Rider Tests are comparable to Second Level or Elementary Tests

Compulsory Movements:
Maximum Time - 4:30- 5:00
Minimum Age of Horse: 6 years

1. **Collected Walk** *(20m minimum)*
2. **Extended Walk** *(20m minimum)*
3. **Collected Walk- Half Pirouette**
4. **Collected Trot - Shoulder-In** *(both reins - 12m minimum)*
5. **Collected Trot including Half Pass** *(both reins)*
6. **Extended Trot**
7. **Collected Canter** *(include an 8m circle)*
8. **Counter Canter** *(both reins - 20m minimum)*
9. **Extended Canter**
10. **Simple Change of Lead** *(both reins)*
11. **Halts and Salutes** *(beginning and end of test)*

* These compulsory moves are based on generally accepted movements. Please be sure to confirm your requirements with your region, type of competition as well as the FEI rule book.

Pony Riders
Acceptable and Unacceptable Movement Chart

Acceptable	Unacceptable
Everything that is not clearly forbidden	Tempi Changes 4s, 3s, 2s, 1s
10m Circle at the Canter	Canter Pirouette
Medium Canter on the Diagonal	Full and Double Walk Pirouettes
Medium Canter and Trot on a 20m Circle	Piaffe
	Passage
	Flying Changes

This Acceptable/Unacceptable Chart is a compilation from several resources. As always, please refer to the complete FEI rule book and your region for a full list of movements.

Rules and Requirements

Juniors Freestyles*
Rider Eligibility

 Junior riders can compete in this division until the end of the calendar year of their 18th birthday.

FEI Junior Rider Tests are comparable to Third Level or Medium Tests

Compulsory Movements:
Maximum Time - 4:30- 5:00
Minimum Age of Horse: 6 years

1. **Collected Walk** *(20m minimum)*
2. **Extended Walk** *(20m minimum)*
3. **Collected Walk- Half Pirouette**
4. **Collected Trot - Shoulder-In** *(both reins - 12m minimum)*
5. **Half Pass in Collected Trot** *(both reins)*
6. **Extended Trot**
7. **Collected Canter**
8. **Half Pass in Collected Canter** *(both reins - 20m minimum)*
9. **Extended Canter**
10. **Flying Change of Lead** *(both reins)*
11. **Halts and Salutes** *(beginning and end of test)*

* These compulsory moves are based on generally accepted movements. Please be sure to confirm your requirements with your region, type of competition as well as the FEI rule book.

124

Junior Riders
Acceptable and Unacceptable Movement Chart

Acceptable	Unacceptable
Everything that is not clearly forbidden	Tempi Changes 4s, 3s, 2s, 1s
Half-Pass Zigzag at the Trot	Canter Pirouette
Half-Pass Zigzag at the Canter with Flying Changes	Piaffe
	Passage
	Full and Double Walk Pirouettes

This Acceptable/Unacceptable Chart is a compilation from several resources. As always, please refer to the complete FEI rule book and your region for a full list of movements.

Rules and Requirements

Young Ride Freestyles*
Rider Eligibility

 Young riders can compete in this division between the ages of 16-21. At age 22, the must compete as an adult.

FEI Young Rider Tests are comparable to FEI Prix St. George

Compulsory Movements:
Maximum Time - 4:30- 5:00
Minimum Age of Horse: 7 years

1. **Collected Walk** *(20m minimum)*

2. **Extended Walk** *(20m minimum)*

3. **Collected Trot -** *(both reins - 12m minimum* ***including shoulder in)***

4. **Collected Trot** *(both reins - including **half pass**)*

5. **Extended Trot**

6. **Collected Canter**

7. **Collected Canter** *(both reins - including half pass)*

8. **Extended Canter**

9. **Flying Change of Lead** *(every fourth stride)*

10. **Flying Change of Lead** *(every third stride)*

11. **Canter Half Pirouette** *(both reins)*

12. **Halts and Salutes** *(beginning and end of test)*

* These compulsory moves are based on generally accepted movements. Please be sure to confirm your requirements with your region, type of competition as well as the FEI rule book.

Young Riders
Acceptable and Unacceptable Movement Chart

Acceptable	Unacceptable
Everything that is not clearly forbidden	Tempi Changes 2s, 1s
	Full Canter Pirouette
	Piaffe
	Passage

This Acceptable/Unacceptable Chart is a compilation from several resources. As always, please refer to the complete FEI rule book and your region for a full list of movements.

Rules and Requirements*

Intermediare 1
Rider Eligibility

Compulsory Movements:
Maximum Time - 4:30- 5:00
Minimum Age of Horse: 7 years

1. **Collected Walk** *(20m minimum)*
2. **Extended Walk** *(20m minimum)*
3. **Collected Trot -** *(both reins - 12m minimum including shoulder in)*
4. **Collected Trot** *(both reins - including **half pass**)*
5. **Extended Trot**
6. **Collected Canter** *(both reins - including **half pass**)*
7. **Extended Canter**
8. **Flying Change of Lead** *(every third stride - 5 consecutive)*
9. **Flying Change of Lead** *(every second stride - 5 consecutive))*
10. **Single Canter Pirouette** *(both reins)*
11. **Halts and Salutes** *(beginning and end of test)*

* These compulsory moves are based on generally accepted movements. Please be sure to confirm your requirements with your region, type of competition as well as the FEI rule book.

Intermediare 1
Acceptable and Unacceptable Movement Chart

Acceptable	Unacceptable
Everything that is not clearly forbidden	Tempi Changes 1s
	Double Canter Pirouette
	Piaffe
	Passage

This Acceptable/Unacceptable Chart is a compilation from several resources. As always, please refer to the complete FEI rule book and your region for a full list of movements.

Rules and Requirements*

Grand Prix
Rider Eligibility

 Compulsory Movements:
Maximum Time - 5:30- 6:00
Minimum Age of Horse: 8 years

1. **Collected Walk** *(20m minimum)*
2. **Extended Walk** *(20m minimum)*
3. **Collected Trot** *(both reins - including **half pass**)*
4. **Extended Trot**
5. **Collected Canter** *(both reins - including **half pass**)*
6. **Extended Canter**
7. **Flying Change of Lead** *(every second stride - 5 consecutive)*
8. **Flying Change of Lead** *(every stride - 9 consecutive))*
9. **Single Canter Pirouette** *(both reins)*
10. **Passage** *(20 steps minimum in one track)*
11. **Piaffe** *(10 steps minimum on a straight line)*
12. **Passage to Piaffe/Piaffe to Passage** *(transitions)*
13. **Halts and Salutes** *(beginning and end of test)*

* These compulsory moves are based on generally accepted movements. Please be sure to confirm your requirements with your region, type of competition as well as the FEI rule book.

Grand Prix
Acceptable and Unacceptable Movement Chart

Acceptable	Unacceptable
Everything that is not clearly forbidden	
Flying Changes on a curved line	
Double Canter Pirouette	Triple Canter Pirouettes
Passage Half Pass	
Piaffe Pirouette	

This Acceptable/Unacceptable Chart is a compilation from several resources. As always, please refer to the complete FEI rule book and your region for a full list of movements.

Appendix 1
Exercise List

Appendix 2
Music Terminology 101 -
A VERY Short Primer on Musical Notation

This section contains a VERY basic introduction to the nature of music as it pertains to its notation and performance. This is not so much meant to teach you music as it is to help you understand some of the jargon that folks will invariably throw into a conversation when talking about music. You can use these little pearls of musical insight to add some credulity to your train of thought when discussing the music you want for your freestyle or practice routine. Chances are, you many never even encounter these terms in the course of your goal to build a musical freestyle. In today's digital domain, music is more readily identified by what is heard than by what is seen or read.

> **Bar** - When a musical composition is written, it is divided into small segments called *bars* or *measures*. They break down the song into ordered chunks of time and beats. Each *bar* or *measure* has 2,3,4 or more beats. This is a simple way of dividing up a piece of music so musicians can keep track of their placement within a given song.

> **Beat** - This is the single most elemental part of any composition, save for the musical notes themselves. The *beat* gives you the indication of rhythm or style for a particular piece of music.

> **Cadence** - This relates to a sequence of notes or chords within a given musical phrase, with emphasis on a particular beat within the *cadence* to indicate its beginning.

> **Clef** - This is a symbol that appears on each musical staff. It tells the musician which

note will be found on each line and space within a given staff. There are three basic clefs:

The Treble Clef 𝄞

The Bass Clef 𝄢

The "C" Clef 𝄡

Each of these denotes where a given root note will be found on the staff *(for example: the treble clef shows where the "G" note can be found, the bass clef indicates where the "F" note can be found, and the "C" clef, well, you get the picture)*. Although the Treble and Bass clefs are pretty much locked in to one position on the staff, the "C" clef can move about, depending on where the composer wants to place the "C" note on the staff *(for purposes of a instrument's or singer's range)*.

Double Time - This phrase indicates that the prevailing rhythm you are hearing is being performed at twice the speed at which it was originally played. For example, if you were clapping a beat at the rate of 50 a minute, the double time for that would be to clap 100 times during the same timeframe. Although *double time* denotes a faster beat, it may not necessarily mean a faster tempo *(how's that for intriguing!)* For example: A piece of music may count off with a BPM of 75. However, if the trot of your horse were measured at 150 BPMs, it would fit the music by virtue of it being twice the speed of the original music *(at 75 BPMs)*. Although you're riding at 150 BPMs, the music still plays at 75 without affecting the original tempo.

Downbeat - The beat within a cadence *(or bar)* that denotes the beginning of the cycle. The main beat in a canter stride is a good example of a *downbeat*.

Harmony - Any time that you hear two different musical lines being performed simultaneously, one of them is described as the *harmony*, while the main line is considered the melody. Although it is often more pleasing to hear harmonies that are performed within the relative pitch of the melody, that is not always the case.

Key Signature - In music, there are three items that a performer needs to know in order to perform a piece of music. The *Key Signature* is probably the most important one - it tells the musician how each of the musical notes on the staff is to sound *(sharp, flat or natural)*.

Measure - Another designation for a *Bar*; both are used interchangeably.

Notes - This is the musical indicator that shows a musician what sound to play, and for how long. Although there are a wide variety of musical notes and types of lengths, the more common ones you are bound to hear about are whole, half, quarter, eighth and sixteenth notes. In a scenario where four beats equal one bar:

Note	Symbol	Beat
Whole	𝅝	4
Half	𝅗𝅥	2
Quarter	𝅘𝅥	1
Eighth	𝅘𝅥𝅮	1/2
Sixteenth	𝅘𝅥𝅯	1/4

Sometimes, a note may be followed by a dot "." - this increases the length of that particular note by half of its value. For example, if a half note is followed by a dot, it is worth 3 beats *(referred to as a "dotted half note")*.

Pitch - This refers to how high or low a musical note sounds within a given range.

Staff - This is where the musical notes for any given composition reside, and which tell the musician which notes to sound off, based on the nature of the clef written at the beginning of the *staff*.

Time Signature - This marker always follows the key signature, and indicates the beat for a particular composition, and the type of note that will fill that particular beat. For example, if you see a "4/4" at the beginning of a musical staff, it simply means that each measure will be 4 beats long, with each beat represented by a quarter note *(which is worth one beat each)*.

Appendix 3
Choosing a Metronome

Metronomes, as explained in **Chapter 3 - Putting It All Together: Riding the Rhythms**, are as varied as the day is long. There are models out there for purists that will count BPMs and nothing else, while others provide rhythmic combinations, pitch control, and stop watches *(to name but a few)*. The following table will give you a basic overview on available features and general pricing *(the latter being an average based on multiple vendors)*. Although our intent here is not to show a preference for any given brand or model, we have rated the ones which, in our opinion, have proven to be a good overall performer in the field. The rating goes from 1 to 5, with "5" being the most functional and "1" being the least.

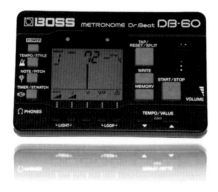

Brand	Model	BPMs	Tempo/Style	Note/Pitch	Timer/Stopwatch	Tap	Tempo Value	Price	Rating	Comments	Sample Picture
Boss	Dr. Beat DB-30	Adjustable by single beat increments	✓	✓	—	✓	✓	$40	5	Probably one of the better choices out there for arena use - easy to handle and store (even has a built-in belt clip)	
Boss	Dr. Beat DB-60	Adjustable by single beat increments	✓	✓	✓	✓	✓	$70	4	Probably has more than you need, but helps to incorporate other useful items such a stopwatch and memory key.	
Korg	MA-30	Adjustable by single beat increments	✓	✓	—	✓	✓	$30	3	Good price for the features, though not build for rugged use.	
Sabine	Metrotune MT9000	Adjustable by preset beat increments only	✓	✓	—	—	—	$30	2	Sturdy metronome; more functional for an instrumentalist or vocalist	
QwikTime	QT-3	Adjustable by preset beat increments only	✓	—	—	—	—	$15	1	Good example of a standard quartz metronome. Again, great for instrumentalists, not very handy for customized BPM selection.	

Appendix 4 -
Audio Equipment Terms of Endearment

As with most things in this world, audio equipment and processes have their own set of terms and phraseologies that tend to throw a wrench into the mix when trying to decipher some of the instructional or procedural guidelines for equipment and such. The following contains a list of those items that we discussed in **Chapter 4**, plus a few more whose intent is to help shed some light on what is often a confusing amalgam of words, wires, and widgets.

Audiocassettes
Also known as compact cassette tapes. Since their inception in 1963, cassettes have been largely eclipsed by the Compact Disk *(CD)*. Interestingly enough, cassettes still enjoy some small marginal advantages over the CD - they are not as susceptible to dust, and can hold more music data than the average CD *(80 minutes for an average CD; 120 minutes for a cassette)*. In a 16-year period from 1990 to 2006, cassette productions dropped from over 400 million *(1990)* to around 700,000 *(2006)*. Although cassettes still remain a viable medium for disseminating music, many recording companies are opting to phase out this medium in favor of the CD.

AUX In
Stands for "Auxiliary Input". Many stereo systems, power amplifiers, and sound equalizers provide this port so that the user may plug in an external sound source for recording or playback.

AUX Out
Stands for "Auxiliary Output". As with the "Auxiliary Input", many stereo systems provide this port so that

the user may plug in an external peripheral for playback or recording.

AWG
Stands for the **American Wire Gauge**, and is an acronym used to express the thickness of a wire's conduc-
tivity by associating a number *(or "gauge")* to a given
thickness. The lower the gauge number, the thicker
the wire, and thus the greater its capacity for passing
an amplified audio signal. Most speaker wire thickness ranges from 12 to 16 gauge.

Boom box
A slang term given to portable stereo systems. Many
of today's portable stereos boast over 150 watts per
channel, removable speakers, built-in equalizers,
stackable CD players, dual tape decks, and stereo FM
radios.

Capstans
In the world of audiocassettes, the *capstans* are the
small, spoke-like spindles onto which you load a cassette into a deck for playing/recording. Many upscale
player/recorder units motorize each of the capstans to
ensure even pressure on the tape for playback, and
for faster and more exacting rewinding/search features.

CD-R
Stands for **C**ompact **D**isk, **R**ead Only. Once data or
music has been recorded onto the surface of the CD,
it cannot be altered or erased. This type of CD is
commonly used for data storage and for creating MP3
or WMA-based music CDs.

CD-R/W
Stands for **C**ompact **D**isk, **R**ead/**W**rite. Unlike the
CD-R disks, data that has been recorded onto the sur-

face of a CD-R/W disk can be altered or erased. This type of CD is used primarily for data storage, and should be not be used to create music CDs, as many players cannot recognize the tracking information for playback.

DAT
Stands for **D**igital **A**udio **T**ape. Introduced commercially in the mid 1980's, DAT recorder/players were able to capture sound at greater *(and lesser)* frequencies than the standard music CD. In 2005, Sony *(the main manufacturer of DATs)* announced that they would discontinue building the devices. Although DATs still find some use in professional film and audio studios, they are no longer considered a viable recording medium in the consumer market.

DAW
Stands for **D**igital **A**udio **W**orkstation. This commonly refers to any computer software that mimics multi-track audio systems designed to record, edit, and play digital audio. Integrated *(or studio)* DAWs are stand-alone systems that perform the same manipulation of digital audio without the use of a computer.

Dolby B & C
Dolby B & C is a standardized noise reduction system used primarily with audiocassettes. Developed by Ray Dolby in 1965 *(and first introduced for the commercial market as Dolby A)*, type B "cleans" up the sound of a recording by providing 10dB *(decibels)* of noise reduction on frequencies above 1kHz. Type C provided up to 20dB of noise reduction in the higher frequency range, but recordings made using Dolby C had to be played back on a system supporting the noise reduction. If not, the quality of the recording was far worse than its original registration. Today, Dolby B & C's analog noise reduction is only

viable for cassette recordings, as digital mediums are of far greater quality and fidelity.

DSP
Stands for **D**igital **S**ignal **P**rocessor, and refers to the process of modifying audio signals digitally. This term is also used when referring to computer software or memory chips that perform digital audio processing *(see DAW)*.

Frequency Response
This term refers to the range between the lowest and highest frequencies that are produced by a piece of audio equipment, and is often used to indicate the accuracy of amplifiers and speakers to reproduce an audio signal.

Line In
Often found on stereo peripherals such as amplifiers, cassette/CD players, graphic equalizers, and other audio-based components. This allows the user to bring a sound signal into the receiving unit.

Line Out
As with *Line In*, this port is found on a wide variety of stereo peripherals. It allows the user to send a sound signal out to another audio peripheral, for example: Using a set of RCA cables to connect an audio signal coming out of a tape deck into a stereo amplifier through the *Line In* port.

Mono/Stereo
Stands for Monoraul/Stereo, and indicates whether an audio signal is split into separate left/right signals that are being played through each respective channel *(stereo)*, or a single signal being played on both the left & right channels *(mono)*.

MP3

The acronym stands for **MPEG-1** *(Moving Pictures Expert Group)* **Audio Layer 3**, and is the digital audio encoding format used for creating music files for digital players such as the iPod, and for encoding computer-based music CDs. Since this format type greatly compresses a song file, it takes up much less space on a device or CD while faithfully maintaining the original file's sound quality.

MP4

The acronym stands for **MPEG-4** *(Moving Pictures Expert Group)* **Part 14**, and is most commonly used for storing both digital audio/video streams and still images.

Ogg Vorbis

This is a compression type used for digital audio & video files. It was developed as a free means for streaming data. *Ogg* refers to the file format itself that provides a number of open source codecs for audio, video, text, and metadata. *Vorbis* is a free and open source audio codec headed by the Xiph.Org Foundation, and was intended to serve as a replacement for MP3.

Phones

This is the port where you plug in your headphones. Little known fact: The term *phones* does relate to the headphone itself, but its origins came from the late 1800's, when the plugs were used in telephone exchange systems. The *headphone* designation merely extended an older term for a newer technology.

Power Amp

This stands for *Power Amplifier*. In very generic terms, an amplifier takes an audio signal and makes it stronger by increasing its amplitude. In the world of musical equipment, a power amp is designed to drive

loudspeakers or other non-powered stereo components. You will often see the term **Pre Amp** *(Pre Amplifier)* floating about as well - this is nothing more
than an amplifier that precedes another amplifier, and
is used to prepare a signal for further amplification.

RCA cables
Also referred to as **RCA jacks** or **phono connectors**.
It's a type of cable connector commonly used with
audio/video equipment. The name **RCA** comes from
the **R**adio **C**orporation of **A**merica, which introduced
the connector design in the early 1940s, and was
used to connect phonograph players to amplifiers.
When high fidelity equipment became popular in the
1950's, RCA plugs started to replace older jack plugs
as the standard for equipment connectivity.

Servomechanisms
Also known as a **servo**. It's an automatic device that
uses error-sensing feedback to correct the performance of a mechanism. CD players have a servo-
mechanism that spins the disk, ensuring that the rota-
tions and balance are kept constant for proper playback. On many upscale cassette tape decks, each
capstan has a servo motor to ensure the tension on
the tape is kept at a constant, and to help avoid tape
clipping during high speed rewinding.

Signal-To-Noise Ratio
Signal-to-noise ratio *(also often seen as SNR)* com-
pares the level of a given signal to the level of the
noise in the background. The higher the ratio, the
less conspicuous the background noise is going to be.

Standard ¼ Stereo Plug
There are several stereo plugs out in use today. The ¼
inch stereo plug is one that is most recognizable -
many headphone *(and ear bud headphone)* manufac-

turers use it today as the connector of choice. Both the ¼ inch and ½ inch plugs *(to name but a couple)* are the most common audio connectors used *(right alongside the RCA connectors)*, and are known as **TRS** *(Tip, Ring, and Sleeve)* **connectors** or **phone plugs**. They were developed in the 19th century for use with telephone switchboards. They are cylindrical in shape, typically with one to three contacts rings *(some types have four)*. When in use on audio cables, the connector with one (1) black contact ring denotes the cable's use for a monoraul *(mono)* signal, while the connector with two (2) black contact rings denotes a stereo cable.

Two-Way & Three-Way Speakers
Since the inception of radio and sound film in the 1930's, quality speakers have played a major part in the listening experience of all audiophiles. Two of the more common types used are the two-way and three-way speakers. The number refers to the amount of cones *(or drivers)* used to recreate sound - a two-way has two speaker cones, and a three-way has three cones. The two-way has one large cone called the *woofer*, and it's used to recreate the lower and mid-range frequencies *(bass)*. The second cone is much smaller, and is called a *tweeter* - it recreates the sounds from the upper frequencies *(treble)*. A three-way speaker has the same configuration, with the exception of a third speaker cone. This one is smaller than the *woofer* yet larger than the *tweeter,* and it handles all the midrange frequencies *(and thus is called the midrange)*. The advantage of a three-way speaker is that the sounds it produces are cleaner and more detailed, since each of the main frequencies are divided among the three speakers cones by means of a *passive crossover circuit,* which splits the sound according to a specific frequency range.

Turntablism
Turntablism is a term given to the art of manipulating sound to create music by using turntables to generate rhythmic sounds along with the help of a mixer.

USB
Stands for **U**niversal **S**erial **B**us, and is a serial bus *(connector)* standard for interfacing computer devices. It was designed to connect peripherals such as a computer mouse, keyboards, printers, digital cameras, etc. to a computer using a single standardized plug. The main advantage that USB provides is that it allows devices to be connected and disconnected without having to reboot the computer *(also known as hot swapping)*.

WMA
Stands for **W**indows **M**edia **A**udio, and is an audio data compression technology developed by Microsoft. It was originally created to be a competitor to the popular MP3 and RealAudio compression formats. Although widely used and supported in mainstream music, it ranks second next to the MP3 format in terms of market support.

Appendix 5:

Choosing Audio Editing Software and Choosing a Digital Audio Workstation (DAW) Software

As we discussed in **Chapter Four**, Digital Audio Workstation *(DAW)* software are programs designed to write/record/ create songs on your computer. They take the sound files created/altered through an audio editor, import them as loops, and then piece them together according to your needs or imagination. There are programs on the market that range in price from affordable to astronomical, and each has a learning curve to overcome - some more daunting than others. Listed on the next page are the Top 5 programs we feel are worth investigating. The table provides a basic overview on essential features and general pricing. As with our table on the audio editing software, our intent is not to show a preference for any given piece of software. Therefore, we have rated each program based on their ease of use and value to you as a prospective song arranger. The rating goes from 1 to 5, with "5" being the most user-friendly and "1" being the least.

Program Name	Input Sound Files	Export Sound Files	Removes Vocals	Smooth Transitions	Multiple Tracks	Effects	Mixdown CD burner	Price	Rating	Comments
ProTools	WAV, MPEG (MP2 & MP3), Ogg, VOX, WMA, RAW	WAV, MP2, MP3, VOX, WMA	---	✓	✓	✓	✓	$300	1	Runs on Windows XP and Mac OS X. Not for the squeamish, ProTools is one of the top DAWs on the market. Short of making a great latte, it's designed to handle the most complex aspects of sound editing/mastering, and its wise to avoid for simple projects unless you're looking to delve into sound synthesis and design in a big way.
SONAR Home Studio 6	WAV, AVI, MIDI, MP3, WMA, WMV	WAV, AVI, MIDI, MP3, WMA, WMV	---	✓	✓	✓	✓	$139	2	Runs on Windows XP, Vista. Made by Roland, this software provides an all-in-one DAW that includes all the features seen in the other packages. As with GarageBand, SONAR is designed more for the seasoned musician looking to establish a serious home-based recording studio.
GarageBand	WAV, AIFF, MPEG (MP2 & MP3), AU, Ogg, VOX, AC3, AAC, CDA, FLAC, WMA, RAW, MPC, AVI	WAV, MP3, Ogg, WMA	---	✓	✓	✓	✓	$79	3	Runs on Mac OS X. Part of Apple's iLife software suite. Great program with an abundance of features that go beyond the needs of the average freestyle arranger. Learning curve is a bit higher than Sony's software, but easily overcome after a few days of work & play.
Acid Music Studio	AIFF, AVI, BMP, GIF, JPG, MIDI, MP3, OGG, PCA, SFA, SWF, TGA, TIF, W64, WAV, WMA	AIFF, ATRAC3, AVI, MP3, OGG, QT, RealAudio™, RealVideo™ W64, WAV, WMA	---	✓	✓	✓	✓	$55	4	Runs on Windows XP or Vista. Ranks a very close second to Sound Forge (both from Sony). Received 2nd Place status because it lacks a vocal line extractor, and because it's geared more so for someone looking to record, edit, and master their own music. Has incredible loop processing capabilities, plus great effects and sound editing features. Also gives you more than what you need to create a great-sounding song file. Learning curve is minimal, though it helps to have a cursory knowledge of basic wave/loop editing.
Sound Forge Audio Studio	AA3, AIFF, AU, AVI, SND, DIG, SD, IVC, MPEG-2* OGG, MPEG-1, OMA, PCA, QT, RAW, SFA, VOX, W64, WAV, WMA, WMV	AA3, AIFF, AU, AVI, DIG, IVC, MP3, MPEG-1&2, OGG, RealAudio® PCA, RAW, RealVideo® QT, VOX, W64, WAV, WMA, WMV	✓	✓	✓	✓	✓	$55	5	Runs on Windows XP or Vista. Overall great program with a wide variety of features to keep your creative streak happy. For the money, it gives you more than what you would need to create a great-sounding song file. Learning curve is minimal, though it helps to have a cursory knowledge of basic wave/loop editing.

Choosing Audio Editing Software

As we discussed in **Chapter Four**, audio editing software are programs designed to manipulate the sound waves you've chosen for your musical freestyle. There are programs out there that range in price from free to affordable, and each has its own set of bells and whistles to fit every need. Listed on the next page are the Top 5 programs we feel are an indispensable part of any good editing studio. The table provides a basic overview on essential features and general pricing. As with our table on the digital audio workstations, our intent is not to show a preference for any given piece of software. Therefore, we have rated each program based on the availability of key components and their ease of use. The rating goes from 1 to 5, with "5" being the most user-friendly and "1" being the least.

Program Name	Input Sound Files	Export Sound Files	Noise Reduction	Tempo Change	Effects	Recording	Price	Rating	Comments
NGWave Audio Editor	WAV, MP3, WMA	WAV, WMA, MP3	✓	✓☞	✓	mic, line in, other sources	$29.95	1	Runs on Windows 98, ME, XP, 2000, Vista. Built-in metronome and audio mixer are nice features. Runs faster than other programs of this type. ☞ - Tempo change is only available through a pitch alteration feature, so be very careful when using this function!
GoldWave Digital Audio Editor	WAV, MP3, Ogg, AIFF, AU, VOX, MAT, SND, VOC, FLAC, Raw Binary Data, Text Data	WAV, MP3, Ogg, WMA	✓	✓	✓	mic, line in, other sources	$45	2	Runs on Windows ME, XP, 2000, Vista. Has more effects features than Dexster, but has more of a learning curve.
Blaze Media Pro	WAV, AIFF, MPEG (MP2 & MP3), AU, Ogg, VOX, AC3, AAC, CDA, FLAC, WMA, RAW, MPC, AVI	WAV, MP3, Ogg, WMA	✓	✓	✓	mic, line in, other sources	$50	3	Runs on Windows 98, SE, 2000, ME, XP, Vista. Solid program with a wealth of features and a clean, easy-to-follow look. Great program, but has more than you would ever need for basic file editing.
Dexster Audio Editor	WAV, AIFF, MPEG (MP2 & MP3), AU, Ogg, VOX, WMA, RAW, MPC, AVI	WAV, MP3	✓	✓	✓	mic, other sources	$40	4	Runs on Windows 98SE, ME, XP, NT 4.0, 2000, 2003, Vista. Program is easy to use for beginners and professionals alike. Also allows you to burn files to a CD.
Audacity	WAV, AIFF, MPEG (MP2 & MP3), AU, Ogg	MP3, WAV, AIFF	✓	✓	✓	mic, line in, other sources	Free*	5	Runs on Windows, Mac OS X, and GNU/Linux platforms. Stable, easy-to-use program with a wealth of features and capabilities. Program provides a quick and easy tool for handling your file editing needs within the freestyle assembly process. Does not support WMA, AAC, or most other proprietary file formats.

Appendix 6
International Associations and Schools

British Dressage Association Rule Book
http://www.britishdressage.co.uk/uploads/File/Rules%20200
8/BD_Rulebook%202008%201.pdf

CADORA Canadian Dressage Association Freestyle Tests
http://www.cadora.ca/Tests/freestyletests.pdf
http://www.cadora.ca/Tests/pasdedeux.pdf

Swedish Dressage Association
http://www2.ridsport.se/

FEI
http://www.fei.org/Disciplines/Dressage/Pages/Default.aspx

FFE French Equestrian Federation
http://www.ffe.com/
http://www.ffe.com/?cat=5&fic=sif/reprises_club_2008.html

SAUMUR (The French National School
http://www.chevalnews.com/

FN (German National Equestrian Federation)
http://www.pferd-aktuell.de

USDF (United States Dressage Federation)
http://www.usdf.org/education/other-programs/musical-freest
yle/index.asp

USEF (United States Equestrian Federation)
http://www.usef.org/Contentpage2.aspx?id=dressage

Dressage Canada
http://www.equinecanada.ca/dressage/index.php?option=co
m_content&task=category&id=1&Itemid=461

BEA -	Bahrain Equestrian Association
BEF -	British Equestrian Federation
CBH -	Confederação Brasileira de Hipismo
CEF -	Cyprus Equestrian Federation
CJF -	Czech Equestrian Federation
CTEA -	Chinese Taipei Equestrian Associatio
DRF -	Dansk Ride Forbund
DRV -	Deutsche Reiterliche Vereinigung e.V.
EC -	Equine Canada
EFA -	Equestrian Federation of Australia Inc.
EFE -	Equestrian Federation of Estonia
EFF -	The Equestrian Federation of Finland
EFI	Equestrian Federation of Ireland
EFS-	Equestrian Federation of Singapore
EFS-	Equestrian Federation of Sloveni
FAS-	Federation Arabe Syrienne des Sports Equestres
FEA-	Federación Ecuestre Argentina
FEC-	Federación Ecuestre de Chile
FEM-	Federación Ecuestre Mexicana
FENA-	Bundesfachverband für Reiten und Fahrenin Oesterreich
FEP -	Federação Equestre Portuguesa
FEP -	Federação Equestre Portuguesa
FEPM -	Federation Equestre de la Principaute de Monaco
FFE -	Federation Francaise d´Equitation
FISE -	Italian Equestrian Federation
FLSE -	Federation Luxembourgeoise des Sports Equestres
FN -	Deutsche Reiterliche Vereinigung
FRBSE -	Federation Royale Belge des Sports Equestres
FSSE -	Federation Senegalaise des Sports Equestres
FSSE -	Federation Suisse des Sports Equestres
GISF -	Grenada International Sports Foundation
HEF -	Hellenic Equestrian Federation

152

HKEF -	Hong Kong Equestrian Federation
IEF -	Isreal Equestrian Federation
KNHS -	Koninklijke Nederlandse Hippische Sportfederatie
NARCI -	The National Association of Riding Clubs in Iceland
NRNEF -	Norges Rytterforbund Norwegian Equestrian Federation
NZEF -	New Zealand Equestrian Federation
PZJ -	Federation Equestre Polonaise
QEF -	Qatar Equestrian Federation
RFHE -	Real Federación Hipica Española
SANEF -	South African National Equestrian Federation
SEF -	Slovak Equestrian Federation
TEFTBF -	Turkish Equestrian Federation Turkiye Binicilik Federasyonu
UAEFED -	United Arab Emirates Equestrian & Racing Federation
UEI -	USA Equestrian, INC

References

Merriam-Webster Online,
http://www.merriam-webster.com/

Ponti, Franco, *Passing Thoughts*, (MarMadd, 1990)

Shakespeare, William, "Richard III", *William Shakespeare: The Complete Works of William Shakespeare*, Gramercy; Unabridged edition, September 8, 1990

Thinkexist.com

Shakespeare, William, "Henry V", *The Complete Works of William Shakespeare*, Gramercy; Unabridged edition, September 8, 1990

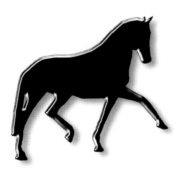

Photo Credits

Cover Photo - EquiChord *(©2006 EquiChord)*

Page 11 - Rebecca Langwost-Barlow and Welfenstein - EquiChord *(©2008 EquiChord)*

Page 38 - Dr. Cesar Parra and Fabio - Susan Stickle *(©2008 Susan J. Stickle)*

Page 69 - Nicole Uphoff-Selke - BS Photography *(©2008 BS Photography)*

Page 106 - Dr. Volker Moritz - Stock Photo

ILLINOIS
Cook
Book

Cooking Across America
Cookbook Collection™

GOLDEN
WEST ☼
PUBLISHERS

Front cover photo courtesy National Pork Producers Council

Printed in the United States of America

2nd printing © 2002

ISBN #1-885590-56-3

Golden West Publishers, Inc.
4113 N. Longview Ave.
Phoenix, AZ 85014, USA

(602) 265-4392

Visit our website: http://www.goldenwestpublishers.com

Illinois Cook Book
Table of Contents

Side Dishes

Breads

Desserts

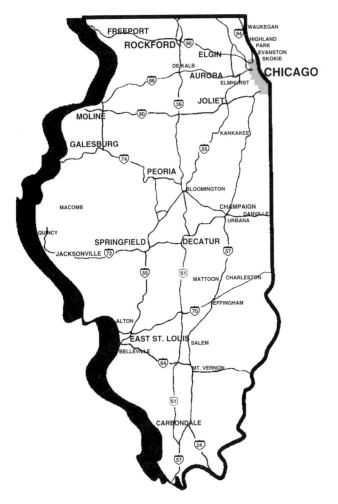

Illinois!

Welcome to the "Land of Lincoln" and the exceptional collection of recipes generously shared by many residents of this great state. Reflecting the diverse cultural and ethnic makeup since its earliest pioneer days to present time, dishes such as *Illinois Country Corn Cakes, Pork Medallions in Herb Sauce* and *German Spice Nuggets* were contributed by chefs, homemakers, bed and breakfast owners and many more.

Enjoy these many tastes of Illinois!

Illinois Facts

Size – 24th largest state with an area of 56,400 square miles
Population – 11,895,849; 6th most populous state *(1997 census)*
State Capital – Springfield
Statehood – December 3, 1818; the 21st state admitted
    to the Union
State Song – "Illinois"
State Nickname – Prairie State
State Motto – *State sovereignty,*
    national union
State Fish – Bluegill
State Fossil – Tully Monster
State Tree – White Oak
State Insect – Monarch Butterfly
State Animal – White-tailed Deer
State Slogan – "Land of Lincoln"
State Mineral – Fluorite
State Name – Algonquin Indian for
    "tribe of superior men"

State Flower
Violet

State Dance
Square Dance

State Bird
Cardinal

Some Famous Illinoisans

Authors/Poets/Writers: Ray Bradbury, Edgar Rice Burroughs, Raymond Chandler, John Dos Passos, Betty Friedan, John Gunther, Ernest Hemingway, James Jones, Frank Norris, Carl Sandburg, Sam Shepard, William L. Shirer, Carl Van Doren, Melvin Van Peebles, Irving Wallace. **Entertainers:** Mary Astor, Jack Benny, Gower Champion, Miles Davis, Walt Disney, Benny Goodman, Charlton Heston, William Holden, Rock Hudson, Burl Ives, Quincy Jones, Bill Murray, Bob Newhart, Richard Pryor, McLean Stevenson, Gloria Swanson, Raquel Welch, Florenz Ziegfeld. **Media:** John Chancellor, William S. Paley, Drew Pearson. **Others:** Jane Addams, Black Hawk, William Jennings Bryan, Jimmy Connors, Richard J. Daly, John Deere, Wyatt Earp, Ulysses S. Grant, George E. Hale, Dorothy Hamill, Wild Bill Hickok, Abraham Lincoln, Robert A. Millikan, Ronald Reagan, Clyde W. Tombaugh, Frank Lloyd Wright.

For more information about Illinois: http://www.state.il.us

Appetizers

Sage Mice

"These are excellent as an unusual appetizer and very special as a garnish on dinner plates. The sage leaves puff up and resemble mice with small tails!"

Maribeth W. King—Mari-Mann Herb Co., Inc., Decatur

4 Tbsp. FLOUR
1 tsp. MARI-MANN® PERFECT HERB SEASONING
SALT to taste
6 Tbsp. WATER
1 EGG YOLK
1 EGG WHITE, stiffly beaten
24 large SAGE LEAVES (with stems)
VEGETABLE OIL

Sift flour, herb seasoning and salt into a bowl; add water and egg yolk and mix to a smooth paste. Cover and let rest for at least 1/2 hour. Gently fold egg white into batter and combine until batter is fluffy. Wash sage leaves and dry thoroughly. Dip leaves in batter and cook in oil until golden brown. If batter loses its airiness before being used up, add a small amount of beaten egg white. Lightly salt.

Hot Chili Dip

"This is especially good for football games! It's a hearty and really tasty dip!"

Jean S. Falk—Woodridge

1 med. ONION, diced
3/4 stick BUTTER
2 pkgs. (8 oz. ea.) CREAM CHEESE, softened
2 cans (15 oz. ea.) CHILI WITH BEANS
1 1/4 tsp. GARLIC POWDER
3/4 tsp. RED PEPPER

Place onion and butter in a large saucepan and cook until onion is clear. Add cream cheese, stirring constantly, until well-blended. Add chili, continuing to stir and cook over low heat. Add garlic and red pepper. Stir until well-blended and thoroughly heated. Serve with nacho chips.

Reuben in the Round

"Carl Buddig & Co. has been manufacturing thin-sliced lunchmeats in the Chicago area for over 50 years!"

Robert Buddig—Carl Buddig & Company, Homewood

18 (3-inch) round RYE, WHEAT or WHITE DINNER ROLLS
6 oz. CARL BUDDIG® CORNED BEEF, chopped
3/4 cup shredded SWISS CHEESE
6 Tbsp. SAUERKRAUT, well-drained
6 Tbsp. MAYONNAISE
3 Tbsp. CHILI SAUCE

Heat oven to 350°. Cut a thin slice from the top of each roll. Hollow out rolls leaving a 1/4-inch shell. Combine beef, cheese, sauerkraut, mayonnaise and chili sauce; mix well. Spoon mixture into rolls and place them on a baking sheet. Bake for 8-10 minutes or until cheese has melted and filling is hot.

Makes 18 sandwiches.

Onion Beef Dip

Sandy Schug—Land O' Frost, Lansing

1 pkg. (2.5 oz.) LAND O' FROST® BEEF
1 pkg. (8 oz.) CREAM CHEESE, softened
1 cup SOUR CREAM
1 pkg. ONION SOUP MIX
1/2 cup chopped CUCUMBER (optional)

Cut beef into small pieces. Place beef in a bowl and add remaining ingredients. Mix well. Refrigerate for 1 hour or more. Serve with crackers.

Black Bean Taco Dip

Maria T. Reid—Reid Foods, Inc., Gurnee

1 jar (12 oz.) MARIA'S STYLE® BLACK BEAN SALSA
1 cup SOUR CREAM
1 cup grated CHEDDAR CHEESE
1 cup grated MONTEREY JACK CHEESE
1 cup GUACAMOLE
1 can (4.25 oz.) chopped BLACK OLIVES
1 lg. TOMATO, chopped

Layer, in order given, in a 9-inch serving dish. Serve with tortilla chips.

Holiday Rollups

Donna Van Eekeren—Land O' Frost, Lansing

1 pkg. (8 oz.) CREAM CHEESE, softened
Dash of GARLIC SALT
1/2 tsp. grated ONION
Dash of WORCESTERSHIRE SAUCE
8 oz. LAND O' FROST® BEEF, PREMIUM HAM,
    or HONEY HAM slices
DILL PICKLES, sliced into spears

In a bowl, blend cream cheese, garlic salt, onion and Worcestershire sauce. Spread mixture on meat slices, add a pickle spear and roll up. Secure each roll with a toothpick. Refrigerate until ready to serve.

Reuben Dip

Sandy Kuck—Land O' Frost, Lansing

3 pkgs. (2.5 oz. ea.) LAND O' FROST® CORNED BEEF
1 can (14 oz.) SAUERKRAUT, drained and rinsed
8 oz. SWISS CHEESE, shredded
4 oz. MILD CHEDDAR CHEESE, shredded
2 GREEN ONIONS, chopped
1 cup MAYONNAISE

Cut corned beef into small pieces and combine in a bowl with remaining ingredients. Pour mixture into an 8 x 8 ungreased pan and bake at 350° for 25-30 minutes. Serve on crackers or rye bread.

Cheese Ball

"This recipe was given to me by my sister-in-law. It is a favorite during the holidays."

Ruby Bryan—Fairview Heights

2 pkgs. (8 oz. ea.) CREAM CHEESE, softened
3-4 GREEN ONIONS, chopped
1 can (8 oz.) PINEAPPLE, drained
1/2 tsp. SEASONED SALT
Ground NUTS

In a bowl, combine all ingredients except nuts. Mix well and form into a large ball. Coat ball with nuts. Serve with crackers.

Smokies

Anne M. Amici—Mascoutah

BACON STRIPS   **SMOKED SAUSAGES,**
BROWN SUGAR   **cocktail size**

Cut bacon strips in half. Make a paste with brown sugar and water. Coat bacon with brown sugar mixture. Wrap bacon around sausages, secure with toothpicks then sprinkle with additional brown sugar. Bake in a 350° oven until bacon has cooked. Drain and sprinkle with more brown sugar. Cook an additional 5-10 minutes.

Fireside's Stuffed Mushrooms

"This has been a family favorite for many years."

Pauletta Hayden—Fireside Inn, Maryville

1 pkg. (8 oz.) CREAM CHEESE, softened
1 lb. BACON, crisply cooked and crumbled
1 tsp. GARLIC POWDER
3 Tbsp. chopped ONION
1 Tbsp. WORCESTERSHIRE SAUCE
4 oz. MOZZARELLA CHEESE, shredded
8 oz. lg. MUSHROOMS

In a bowl, mix first 6 ingredients together. Remove stems from mushrooms and stuff with cream cheese mixture. Place mushrooms, stuffing side up, under broiler and cook until lightly browned.

Chicken Liver Paté

"In Belgium, food is often served with one of the 400 different kinds of beers produced in the country."

Bonnie Taets Newman—Center for Belgian Culture of Western Illinois, Moline

1/2 lb. CHICKEN LIVERS, rinsed and drained
1/2 cup WHITE WINE
8 Tbsp. BUTTER, softened
1 Tbsp. PORT WINE
SALT and PEPPER to taste
Pinch of NUTMEG

Bring chicken livers and white wine to a boil in a small saucepan. Cook over medium heat for 3-4 minutes. Drain and place in a food processor. Purée until smooth. Place mixture in a small bowl and stir in remaining ingredients. Refrigerate until ready to serve.

Burrito Dumplings

"My 9-year-old grandson, Nicholas Diebel, won 1st prize in a Pillsbury bake-off contest with this recipe."

Mrs. Virginia Herzog—Bensenville

1 tube (8 oz.) refrigerated PILLSBURY® CRESCENT ROLLS
1 cup cooked GROUND BEEF, flavored with taco seasoning
1 cup cooked RICE
1 cup LAS PALMAS® REFRIED BEANS
1/2 cup shredded CHEDDAR CHEESE

Preheat oven to 400°. Spray a 9 x 13 baking dish with nonstick cooking spray. Dust a flat surface with flour; unroll the dough and divide it on dividing lines into 4 squares. Turn squares so that both sides are floured. Roll out each to a 6-inch square. Combine beef, rice and beans. Place about 2 tablespoons of meat mixture in the center of each square. Sprinkle with a tablespoon of cheese. Dampen edges of each square and then bring opposite corners up and over the mix. Pinch to seal. Place dumplings in baking dish and bake for 25 minutes or until golden brown. Serve with sides such as salsa or guacamole.

Vegetables Alla Bagna Caöda

"From the 'Tornaco in Cucina Italian Recipes' cookbook which is sold every year at our Herrinfesta Italiana."

Jeanne Fisher—Herrin Chamber of Commerce, Herrin

7 oz. SALTED ANCHOVIES
3 1/2 oz. fresh GARLIC CLOVES, thinly sliced
1 cup EXTRA-VIRGIN OLIVE OIL
3 Tbsp. BUTTER or 3 1/2 oz. fresh CREAM

Rinse anchovies, dry and remove the bones then chop. In a small skillet, place anchovies, garlic and olive oil over very low heat, for about 20 minutes, stirring occasionally. Stir in butter (or cream) and serve hot in individual bowls as a dipping sauce. Serve with a variety of **fresh, raw VEGETABLES.**

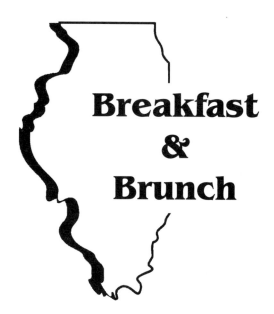

Breakfast & Brunch

Decadent French Toast

"This recipe is from 'Table of Plenty,' a fund-raising cookbook put together by Christ the King Parish in Springfield."

Kathryn Rem—Food Editor, *The State Journal-Register,* Springfield

2 Tbsp. LIGHT CORN SYRUP	5 EGGS
5 Tbsp. BUTTER	1 1/2 cups MILK
1 cup packed BROWN SUGAR	1 tsp. VANILLA
1 cup chopped PECANS	CINNAMON
1 loaf FRENCH BREAD, sliced	WHIPPED CREAM
into 1 1/2-inch thick slices	STRAWBERRIES

This must be made the day before serving. In a saucepan, cook syrup, butter and sugar until bubbly. Pour into a 9 x 13 pan. Generously sprinkle chopped pecans over syrup mixture. Arrange bread slices over syrup/nut layer. Beat together eggs, milk and vanilla. Pour over bread. Cover and refrigerate overnight. Bake at 350° for 45 minutes and then immediately invert each portion onto warm serving plates. Sprinkle cinnamon over top of each serving and garnish with whipped cream and strawberries, if desired.

Jewish Coffee Cake

"When I was little, my grandma let me help her bake this cake. Now I am 13 and can make it by myself."

Christie Brinkmann—Dupo

Cake:
- 1 pkg. (18.5 oz.) WHITE CAKE MIX
- 1 pkg. (3.5 oz.) INSTANT VANILLA PUDDING MIX
- 1/2 cup SALAD OIL
- 1 cup SOUR CREAM
- 4 EGGS, unbeaten

Topping:
- 1/3 cup SUGAR
- 1/2 cup chopped PECANS
- 1 tsp. CINNAMON

Combine all cake ingredients and pour into a well-greased tube pan. Combine topping ingredients and swirl into cake batter with a fork. Bake at 350° for 50-55 minutes.

My Favorite Pancakes

Donna Wilkerson—Dahlgren

- 1 1/4 cups FLOUR
- 2 1/2 tsp. BAKING POWDER
- 1 Tbsp. SUGAR
- 3/4 tsp. SALT
- 1 EGG, beaten
- 1 cup MILK
- 3 Tbsp. melted SHORTENING

In a bowl, combine dry ingredients. Add balance of ingredients and blend. Melt a small amount of shortening in a skillet to barely cover bottom. Drop batter by tablespoons into the heated skillet. Brown on both sides.

My Sister's Coffee Cake

Dennis W. Page—Bloomington

- 1 cup SUGAR
- 2 EGGS
- 1/2 cup MILK
- 2 cups FLOUR
- 1/2 tsp. SALT
- 1 tsp. BAKING POWDER
- 1/2 cup packed BROWN SUGAR
- 1 tsp. CINNAMON
- 1/2 cup melted BUTTER

In a bowl, combine all ingredients together. Pour batter into a 9-inch baking pan and bake at 375° for 20-30 minutes.

Caramel-Apple French Toast

"This is a great favorite of our guests!"

Patty Rinehart—River House Bed & Breakfast, Rockford

1 cup packed BROWN SUGAR
3 Tbsp. LIGHT CORN SYRUP
6 Tbsp. BUTTER
1/2 cup whole PECANS
3 DELICIOUS APPLES,
   peeled and sliced
1/3 cup WATER
1/2 tsp. CINNAMON
3 Tbsp. SUGAR
1 Tbsp. LEMON JUICE
1 Tbsp. CORNSTARCH
12 oz. CREAM CHEESE, softened

12 (1-inch thick) slices
   FRENCH BREAD
6 EGGS
1 cup MILK
1 cup WHIPPING CREAM
   or HALF and HALF
1 Tbsp. VANILLA
2 tsp. CINNAMON
POWDERED SUGAR
WHIPPED CREAM
Chopped PECANS
CINNAMON or NUTMEG

Generously grease a 9 x 13 glass baking dish. In a saucepan, combine brown sugar, syrup and butter and boil for 1 minute. Spread over bottom of baking dish. Sprinkle with pecans. In a saucepan, combine apples, water, cinnamon, sugar and lemon juice. Cook over medium heat, stirring constantly, until apples begin to soften. Add cornstarch and continue to stir until thickened. Remove from heat. Thickly spread cream cheese over 6 slices of bread and place in a single layer, cream cheese side up, on caramel mixture in pan. Distribute apple mixture over the bread. Cover with remaining 6 slices of bread. In a bowl, blend together eggs, milk, cream, vanilla and cinnamon and then gently pour over bread layers. Cover and refrigerate overnight. Remove cover and bake at 350° for 60 minutes or until brown and slightly puffy. Immediately invert each serving onto serving plates, sprinkle with powdered sugar, top with whipped cream and garnish with pecans, cinnamon or nutmeg.

Serves 6.

Potato Pancakes

"This recipe came from a 1910 cookbook. My family just loves these pancakes."

Florence Wolters—Albers

6 lg. POTATOES, peeled and grated
2 EGGS, beaten
1/2 cup FLOUR
1 tsp. BAKING POWDER
SALT and PEPPER to taste

In a bowl, combine all ingredients and stir briskly. Drop from a tablespoon into about one-inch of hot cooking oil in a skillet. Brown both sides. Serve hot with butter and syrup.

Country Corn Cakes

Donna Wilkerson—Dahlgren

1 can (11 oz.) WHOLE KERNEL CORN, drained
1 EGG, well-beaten
SALT and PEPPER to taste
FLOUR, enough to make a thick batter

In a bowl, combine all ingredients, mixing well. Heat cooking oil in a skillet and carefully drop batter by tablespoons into the hot oil. Cook on both sides until golden brown.

Belgian Waffles

"Belgian waffles are usually served as a dessert or afternoon treat. The Center holds a waffle breakfast the 1st Saturday of every month."

Dolores Bultinck—Center for Belgian Culture of Western Illinois, Moline

2 cups FLOUR
3 tsp. BAKING POWDER
3/4 tsp. SALT
6 Tbsp. BUTTER, softened
2 Tbsp. SUGAR
3 EGGS
1 1/2 cups MILK

In a bowl, mix all ingredients together. Bake in a hot waffle iron. Serve with syrup, powdered sugar, whipped cream, strawberries or fruit of choice.

Apple Pancakes with Spicy Yogurt & Cider Syrup

"Cider syrup is simply an apple cider reduction. The apple cider is cooked down to a thick amber syrup which concentrates the natural sugar and rich apple flavor."

Drusilla Banks—University of Illinois Extension, Urbana-Champaign

2 cups SKIM MILK
2 EGGS, slightly beaten
6 Tbsp. CHUNKY APPLESAUCE
2 cups WHOLE-WHEAT PANCAKE MIX
CANOLA OIL
CINNAMON

In a large bowl, combine milk, eggs and applesauce. Stir in pancake mix. Mix enough to moisten; do not overmix. If the batter is too thick add a little water. Heat a large nonstick skillet or griddle over medium heat. When skillet is hot, coat lightly with a small amount of oil. Add batter to skillet, making medium pancakes (about 1/2 cup batter per pancake). Cook until golden brown on both sides. Place on serving plates. Drizzle with **Cider Syrup** and top with a dollop of **Spicy Yogurt**. Garnish with a sprinkle of cinnamon.

Serves 4.

Cider Syrup & Spicy Yogurt

6 cups APPLE CIDER
1 cup PLAIN YOGURT
1/2 tsp. CINNAMON
1/4 tsp. NUTMEG
6 Tbsp. CHUNKY APPLE-SAUCE

Pour apple cider into a 3-quart saucepan. Place the pan over high heat and bring to a boil. Reduce heat to a very slow boil and cook for about 30 minutes or until the cider is reduced to one cup. Set aside. In a small bowl, combine yogurt, cinnamon, nutmeg and applesauce. Cover and refrigerate.

Lynfred's Oven-Baked Omelet

"Lynfred Winery has been pairing its wine with food recipes for more than 10 years. As Illinois' oldest winery, Lynfred strives to enhance the culinary experience for our customers."

Fred Koehler—Lynfred Winery, Roselle

2 RED BELL PEPPERS
8 BACON SLICES
10 lg. EGGS
1/2 cup MILK
3 Tbsp. LYNFRED® SEYVAL BLANC
1/4 cup fresh BASIL, chopped or 1 Tbsp. dried, crumbled
1/2 tsp. SALT
1/4 tsp. freshly ground BLACK PEPPER

Preheat oven to 350°. Halve and seed the red peppers. Cut each half into thin horizontal strips. Cut bacon into 1-inch pieces. Sauté bacon over medium heat until crisp and then transfer to paper towels; keep warm. Reserve bacon drippings in pan. Add peppers to the pan and cook over medium heat until softened, about 3 minutes. In a bowl, beat eggs until smooth; stir in milk and wine. Beat until just incorporated. Do not overbeat. Stir in basil, salt and pepper. Divide peppers among shallow ramekins or small soufflé dishes. Add egg mixture, filling to 1/2-inch from the top. Set ramekins (or dishes) in a deep baking tray. Place tray in oven; add water to 1/4-inch in depth and bake until set, about 20 minutes. Top each serving with bacon; serve immediately.

Serves 4.

Illinois Wineries

Grape growers are located in 34 Illinois counties. Their vineyards produce a variety of fine wines including reds, blushes and whites. Also produced are award-winning fruit wines.

French Toast

"This is a family favorite, especially on Sunday mornings before going to church."

Mrs. Jeffery J. Brinkmann—Dupo

3 EGGS	**1 1/2-2 cups MILK**
1/4 cup SUGAR	**SLICED BREAD**
1 heaping tsp. FLOUR	**POWDERED SUGAR**
1 tsp. VANILLA	**SYRUP**

Mix all ingredients together and beat well. Dip each slice of bread in mixture and cook in a skillet that has been sprayed with a nonstick coating. Cook both sides until golden brown. Place on serving plates and sprinkle with powdered sugar or syrup.

Note: Using day old bread provides the best results!

Dot's Buttermilk Pancakes

"This recipe was given to me by an old friend who was born in the late 1800s. It is one of our favorite breakfast dishes."

Virginia McCord—Wayne City

For each **1 cup of FLOUR** add:

- **1 tsp. BAKING SODA**
- **1/4 tsp. SALT**
- **1 EGG**
- **1 tsp. SUGAR**
- **1 tsp. COOKING OIL**
- **1 cup BUTTERMILK**

Lightly blend ingredients. Add **MARGARINE** to a skillet and cook each pancake until golden brown on both sides.

Scottish Eggs
with Dijon Sauce

"Our Bed and Breakfast is in a 113-year-old renovated barn that has been kept as authentic as possible. Scottish eggs are often found in Scottish 'pubs'. There, they are often deep-fried and served cold! We changed things a bit and serve them hot to our guests."

Karen M. Sharp—The Barn of Rockford Bed & Breakfast, Rockford

3/4-1 lb. GROUND SAUSAGE
1/2 cup dried BREAD CRUMBS
1 EGG
2-3 Tbsp. chopped ONION
1 Tbsp. dried PARSLEY
1/4 tsp. SALT
1/2 tsp. SAGE
1/4 tsp. THYME
4 HARD-BOILED EGGS, shelled

Combine all ingredients, except eggs, in a bowl. Divide the mixture into fourths. Take one fourth, lay it in your hand and flatten until it is large enough to surround a boiled egg. Place egg in flattened mixture, seal well and place in a baking dish. Cover and bake at 350° for 45 minutes to an hour. Remove cover the last 10 minutes or so to brown. Serve with ***Dijon Sauce.***

Dijon Sauce

2 Tbsp. DIJON MUSTARD
1-2 Tbsp. SUGAR
1 1/2 Tbsp. VINEGAR
1/2 tsp. SALT
1 tsp. chopped FRESH DILL, less if dried
1/3 cup CANOLA OIL

Whisk together the first 5 ingredients. Gradually whisk in the oil. Pour into a glass jar. May be refrigerated up to 5 days.

Soups & Salads

Morel & Hazelnut Soup

"Morel mushrooms are a highly sought-after culinary delicacy and are indigenous to the entire state of Illinois. The morel mushroom festival is held the 3rd weekend in April at Jonesboro."

Carol Hoffman—Southernmost Illinois Tourism Bureau, Ullin

3 tsp. BUTTER	1/4 tsp. OREGANO
1 med. ONION, chopped	1 BAY LEAF
2 stalks CELERY, coarsely chopped	2 cloves GARLIC, minced
1 LEEK, chopped	2 Tbsp. melted BUTTER
3 Tbsp. FLOUR	1/3 cup WHITE WINE
4 cups POULTRY STOCK	1 cup HALF and HALF
1/2 tsp. THYME	2/3 cup finely ground toasted HAZELNUTS
1/4 tsp. BASIL	1 lb. MOREL MUSHROOMS

In a skillet, melt butter and sauté onion and celery. Add leek and flour; cook for five minutes. Add poultry stock, stirring with a wire whisk. Add spices and garlic; bring to a boil. Reduce heat and simmer for 30 minutes. Remove from heat and take out bay leaf. Pass mixture through a sieve or food mill. Return to saucepan and simmer over medium heat while adding remaining ingredients.

Serves 6.

Pat's Garlic-Chicken Vegetable Soup

"This is an original recipe that I developed. It hits the spot on cold winter nights and smells great while cooking, too!"

Patricia S. Blair—East Peoria

3 Tbsp. MARGARINE
1/2 lg. ONION, chopped
6 cloves GARLIC, crushed
4 med. CARROTS, diced
2 stalks CELERY (tops included), chopped
4 med. POTATOES, diced
1 med. SWEET POTATO, diced
1/4 cup PARSLEY FLAKES
SALT and PEPPER to taste
8 cups WATER
4 med. boneless CHICKEN BREASTS, cut into 1/2-inch cubes
1/2 cup SOY SAUCE

In a large soup kettle, place margarine, onion and garlic; sauté. Add carrots and celery; cook over low heat, covered, stirring occasionally. Add potatoes. Stir together; add parsley flakes, salt and pepper. When onion is clear, add enough water to fill pan. Add chicken breasts and soy sauce. Bring to a boil and simmer for 1 hour, or until chicken is very tender.

Historic Route 66

Beginning in Chicago, Route 66 heads south-west cutting through rich agricultural lands. Corn, oats and soybean crops abound along with large hog and cattle farms. Bordered by cities such as Bloomington and Springfield, this Illinois portion of the highway displays much of the heritage of the Central Heartland. Heading further south-west Route 66 exits the state at East St. Louis by crossing the Mississippi River.

Curlicue Pasta Salad

"This is a tangy, refreshing salad. The homemade marinade is worth the extra effort."

Virginia Shuemaker—Neoga

1 pkg. (16 oz.) TRI-COLORED ROTINI PASTA
1 3/4 cups OIL
2/3 cup WHITE WINE VINEGAR
2 Tbsp. LEMON JUICE
1 Tbsp. DIJON MUSTARD
2 cloves GARLIC, minced
1 1/2 tsp. SALT
1/2 tsp. PEPPER
1/2 tsp. dried OREGANO
1/4 tsp. SUGAR
1 1/2 cups sliced MUSHROOMS
1 1/2 cups sliced ZUCCHINI
1 1/2 cups sliced RED or GREEN BELL PEPPER
1/2 cup finely chopped PARSLEY
1/2 cup chopped GREEN ONIONS, tops included

Cook pasta according to package directions; drain. Place in a large salad bowl. Whisk the next 9 ingredients together. Pour over warm pasta; stir to coat. Add remaining ingredients. Cover and refrigerate for 6 hours, or overnight. Stir before serving.

Poppy Seed Dressing

"My mother, Mabel, made this often and shared it with me. Now it is a favorite house dressing at the inn."

Nina Heymann—Oscar Swan Country Inn, Geneva

1/2 ONION, chopped
2 cups OIL
1 1/2 cups SUGAR
2/3 cup RICE WINE VINEGAR

1 tsp. SALT
1 tsp. DRY MUSTARD
1 tsp. POPPY SEEDS

Put the onion into a blender and blend for about 20 seconds. Place all remaining ingredients in the blender and mix for about 45 seconds or until well combined. Refrigerate.

Oxtail Soup

"This recipe dates back to the days when Chicago was known for its stockyards. My mother used to go to the market and buy fresh oxtails for this soup."

Frank J. Boblak—Elk Grove Village

1 OXTAIL, cut up
2 Tbsp. CANOLA OIL
1 ONION, chopped
2 qts. WATER
1/2 cup BARLEY
1 clove GARLIC, minced
2 cups chopped CELERY
1 tsp. dried PARSLEY FLAKES
1/2 tsp. BASIL LEAVES

1/2 BAY LEAF
2 CARROTS, diced
1 can (16 oz.) TOMATOES, cut up
3 Tbsp. VINEGAR
1 PARSNIP, diced
1 TURNIP, diced
2 Tbsp. SUGAR
1/2 tsp. BLACK PEPPER

In a skillet, brown oxtail pieces in oil. Set aside. In the same skillet, sauté onion until tender. Place meat in a large pot and add 2 quarts of water. Bring to a rapid boil. Skim surface and then reduce heat to low. Add sautéed onion, barley, garlic, celery, parsley, basil and bay leaf. Cook for 1 1/2 hours. Add carrots, tomatoes, vinegar, parsnip, turnip, sugar and black pepper. Cook an additional 1 1/2-2 hours. Remove bay leaf. Serve with rye bread, horseradish and dill pickles.

Chicago

Founded in 1830, Chicago has become a thriving metropolis of nearly three million people. It is bordered by Lake Michigan to the east and "Chicagoland", an array of cities, towns and villages far to the north, south and west. This vast area offers a diverse selection of things to do and see from celebrated architecture, museums, and historical sites to varied cultural, shopping and ethnic dining experiences. Famous for its deep-dish pizza, Sears Tower and Chicago Cubs, to name only a few, Chicago truly offers "something for everyone".

Chicken Salad

"I've been using this recipe for years and we all love it. It's elegant, yet easy to make."

Janet O'Donnell—Collinsville

2 1/2 cups diced CHICKEN
1 cup finely diced CELERY
1 cup quartered GRAPES
3/4 cup chopped NUTS
1 tsp. SALT

3/4 cup MAYONNAISE
1/2 cup SOUR CREAM
3/4 tsp. DILL WEED
1 Tbsp. chopped ONION

Mix all ingredients together, stirring well. Spread on croissants to serve.

Did You Know?

The "World's Largest Catsup Bottle" can be found in Collinsville. The Brooks Catsup Bottle, constructed as a water tower in 1949 in honor of the Brooks Catsup Company is 170 feet high!

Dottie's Traveling Salad

"This is a great salad to make the day before a picnic and take along. Don't add dressing until ready to serve."

Dorothy J. Kennedy Brooks—Collinsville

1 sm. head CAULIFLOWER, chopped
1 sm. head BROCCOLI, chopped
1/3 cup chopped ONION
1 cup chopped TOMATOES
4 HARD-BOILED EGGS, shelled and chopped
1 cup MAYONNAISE
1/3 cup SUGAR
1/4 cup VINEGAR
6 slices BACON, cooked and crumbled

In a large bowl, combine vegetables and eggs. In a small bowl, blend together mayonnaise, sugar and vinegar; add bacon. Cover both and refrigerate until ready to use.

Broccoli-Raisin Salad

"This is a great salad to bring along for a picnic."

Patty Peek—Leu Civic Center, Inc., Mascoutah

2 cups BROCCOLI FLORETS
8 slices BACON, cooked and crumbled
1/2 cup WHITE RAISINS

Toss all ingredients together in a large bowl. Top with *Apple Cider Dressing.*

Apple Cider Dressing

1 cup MAYONNAISE
1/4 cup SUGAR
2 tsp. APPLE CIDER VINEGAR

Mix ingredients together and pour over salad, tossing well. Sprinkle with **shredded CHEESE.**

Grandma's Potato Salad

"This has been handed down through several generations. It's a family favorite."

Marian Mahler—Woodridge

7 med. POTATOES
2-3 stalks CELERY, chopped
1/2 cup chopped ONION
3 HARD-BOILED EGGS
MAYONNAISE to taste

SALT and PEPPER to taste
2-4 slices BACON
1/4 cup VINEGAR
1 Tbsp. FLOUR
2-3 tsp. SUGAR

Cook potatoes in jackets, peel and dice. Shell and chop the eggs. In a large bowl, combine potatoes with celery, onion, eggs, mayonnaise, salt and pepper. Fry bacon until crisp; drain on paper towels and crumble when cool. Add to potato mixture. Pour off half of bacon drippings and add vinegar, flour and sugar. Stir until thick. Pour hot mixture over salad; mix well.

Marinated Chicken-Rice Salad

"I teach cooking classes and write a weekly food column for our local newspaper."

Carol J. Moore—Galesburg

1 pkg. (1.2 oz.) GOOD SEASON'S® ITALIAN DRESSING MIX
1 can (13.75 oz.) water-packed ARTICHOKES, drained and cut up
2 pkgs. (5.4 oz.) UNCLE BEN'S® WILD RICE MIX
2 cups chopped CELERY
1 cup MAYONNAISE
1 jar (4 oz.) PIMENTO, sliced
1 cup chopped GREEN BELL PEPPER
1-5 WHOLE CHICKEN BREASTS, cooked, cooled and diced
1 lb. fresh MUSHROOMS, sliced

Mix Italian dressing according to package instructions, add artichokes and let marinate. Cook rice according to package directions, using 1/2 cup less water than called for. Cool. In a large bowl, combine Italian dressing, artichokes, celery, mayonnaise, pimento and bell pepper. Add chicken and rice. Let mixture marinate overnight. One hour before serving, gently toss sliced mushrooms with salad.

Raspberry Dressing

"My friend, Jan Palermo, gave me this recipe. She added my jalapeño jam to it and I have been told it tastes great!"

Maria T. Reid—Reid Foods, Inc., Gurnee

12 Tbsp. OIL
4 Tbsp. BALSAMIC VINEGAR
2 Tbsp. RED WINE VINEGAR
3 cloves GARLIC, sliced
1 rounded Tbsp. MARIA'S STYLE® RASPBERRY JALAPEÑO JAM
SALT and PEPPER to taste

Combine all ingredients, mix well; let sit several hours or overnight.

Confetti Slaw

Pam Berek—Quig's Orchard and Country Store, Mundelein

1 can (15 oz.) chopped SAUERKRAUT, drained
1/2 cup QUIG'S® PEPPER RELISH
1 cup QUIG'S® VIDALIA SWEET ONION RELISH
1 med. GREEN BELL PEPPER, chopped
1 Tbsp. SUGAR

Combine all ingredients in a large bowl and mix well. Cover and refrigerate overnight. Keeps well for a week or more.

Editors Note: Last fall, Quig's Orchard donated over 1400 pounds of apples in the Share the Harvest Program developed by the North American Farmers Direct Marketing Association to help feed the hungry."

Overnight 7-Layer Salad

"This salad is in demand at every holiday gathering."

Susan Beall-Geever—Schiller Park

1 med. head LETTUCE, torn
1 med. head CAULIFLOWER, cut into small pieces
2 cups MIRACLE WHIP®
1 sm. RED ONION, sliced
1 lb. BACON, cooked and crumbled
1/2 cup PARMESAN CHEESE
1/3 cup SUGAR

In a large mixing bowl, layer ingredients in the order listed. Cover and refrigerate overnight. Toss well before serving.

Perky Pink Fruit Dressing

"Use as a fruit dip or pour over fruit or mixture of fruits. This is especially good over bananas!"

Pam Berek—Quig's Orchard and Country Store, Mundelein

Combine equal parts of **MAYONNAISE** and **SOUR CREAM**. Add **1 1/2 Tbsp. QUIG'S® JALAPEÑO PEPPER JELLY** for each cup of mixture made.

Main Dishes

Pork Medallions in Herb Sauce

"My husband, Ed, and I raise hogs in northern Illinois. I modeled this recipe after a dish he often ordered from a favorite restaurant. Now he likes this version so well that he no longer orders it when we go out to eat!"

Darla J. Arndt—Malta

2 lbs. PORK TENDERLOIN MEDALLIONS	1 Tbsp. THYME
4 Tbsp. BUTTER	1 Tbsp. BASIL
2 cloves GARLIC, minced	1/2 pt. WHIPPING CREAM
1 Tbsp. FLOUR	1/2 pt. HALF and HALF
1/2 tsp. SALT	EGG NOODLES, cooked

In a large skillet, cook medallions to desired doneness. Remove from pan and set aside; keep warm. Add butter and garlic to drippings in skillet and simmer for one minute. Stir in flour. Add remaining ingredients (except noodles) and cook until reduced by one-fourth. Add meat to sauce; heat and then serve over noodles.

Roast Pheasant with Brandy & Cream

"Our family used this recipe to promote the serving of game farm pheasants in Lockport and Chicago. The Czimer family started a 'pheasant for food' farm operation in the Lockport area in the 1950s and sold game in Chicago until the 1970s when the business moved to Lockport."

Richard Czimer, Jr—Czimer's Game & Sea Foods, Inc., Lockport

3 PHEASANTS
6 slices BACON
4 Tbsp. BUTTER
2 Tbsp. minced ONION
1 clove GARLIC, crushed
1/2 cup BRANDY
2 cups CHICKEN STOCK

1/2 tsp. freshly ground
  BLACK PEPPER
1 tsp. SALT
1 pint HEAVY CREAM
1/4 cup PREPARED
  HORSERADISH

Cover breasts of pheasants with bacon slices and tie up so they will not lose shape. Brown in iron frying pan with butter. Add onion and garlic and sauté until soft. After birds are browned, place in a baking pan with sautéed onion, garlic and juices from frying pan. In an open, safe area of your kitchen, pour brandy over birds and light. When flame dies, add chicken stock, pepper and salt. Roast, uncovered, in a 375° oven for half an hour, basting frequently. Add cream and horseradish to sauce, continue roasting for 15 minutes, still basting frequently. Serve birds on heated platter with sauce around them.

Did You Know?

- *The University of Chicago was the birthplace of atomic energy.*
- *Fort Dearborn, built in 1803 and destroyed by Indians in 1812, developed into Chicago.*
- *The Great Chicago Fire in 1871 destroyed much of the city and left 90,000 persons homeless.*
- *John Deere developed and built the steel plow at Grand Detour.*
- *George M. Pullman built the first railroad sleeping car at Bloomington in 1858.*

Venison Chili

"The rolling, wooded hills of southern Illinois are rich with hunting opportunities."

Carol Hoffman—Southernmost Illinois Tourism Bureau, Ullin

2 lbs. cubed VENISON
2 med. ONIONS, chopped
1 cup finely chopped GREEN BELL PEPPER
4 cups WATER
2 cubes BEEF BOUILLON
1 can (16 oz.) TOMATOES, undrained
1 1/2 tsp. VINEGAR
1 tsp. WORCESTERSHIRE SAUCE
1 Tbsp. CHILI POWDER
2 tsp. ground CUMIN
Pinch of OREGANO
Pinch of BASIL
1 tsp. CAYENNE PEPPER
1/2 tsp. GARLIC POWDER
2 BAY LEAVES

Combine venison, onion, bell pepper and water in a large saucepan. Simmer until meat is tender. Add remaining ingredients. Simmer until flavors have blended. Remove bay leaves before serving.

Golconda

Golconda, in Pope County, is known as the Deer Capital of Illinois. This historic river town is a gateway to the sprawling Shawnee National Forest with its spectacular scenery and forests. The Buel House, built here in 1837, is where freshly cooked pumpkin was given to the starving Cherokees as they passed on the famous "Trail of Tears" march. It represents one of the few places the Cherokees are known to have received kind treatment during their sad walk to Oklahoma.

Pork Loin with Wild Rice & Apricot Stuffing

"Here in Henry County, we produce a lot of pork. At one time, we were the highest pork-producing county in the world. I have prepared this dish for special family meals many times. It is country elegance at its best!"

Carrie Sanden-Roe—Blue Moon Farm, Coal Valley

1 cup WILD RICE
4 lbs. BONELESS PORK LOIN
SALT and PEPPER to taste
GARLIC POWDER to taste
1 med. ONION, chopped
1 cup coarsely chopped,
    dried APRICOTS
1/2 cup chopped PARSLEY
1/2 cup minced CELERY
1/2 tsp. SAGE
1/2 tsp. THYME
1 EGG, well-beaten
1/2 lb. BACON
PARSLEY for garnish

Cook and drain wild rice. Butterfly the pork loin by slashing down the center lengthwise, cutting almost all the way through, then open the two halves and lay flat. Sprinkle with salt, pepper and garlic powder. Blend together the remaining ingredients except bacon. Pile half of the mixture in the center of the pork loin and roll up lengthwise. Tie with string at 2-inch intervals. Line a roasting pan with foil; grease foil. Spoon remaining stuffing down the center of the pan to make a bed for the meat; place pork loin on top. Roast in a 350° oven for 1 1/2 hours. Remove from oven and carefully take off strings. Place bacon strips over meat. Bake another 1/2 hour, basting with pan juices. Place loin on a serving platter and surround it with stuffing and pan juices. Garnish with parsley. Cut into thick slices to serve.

Springfield Horseshoes

"Horseshoe sandwiches are extremely popular in the Springfield area where they can be found on menus in many restaurants."

Kathryn Rem—Food Editor, *The State Journal-Register,* Springfield

1/2 cup BUTTER
1/4 cup FLOUR
1 tsp. SALT
1/2 tsp. freshly ground BLACK PEPPER
2 cups HALF and HALF
1/2 tsp. CAYENNE PEPPER
2 cups shredded CHEDDAR CHEESE
8 slices BREAD, toasted
HAM, CHICKEN, or TURKEY, sliced or shaved, or cooked
    GROUND BEEF PATTIES
FRENCH FRIES, cooked

Melt butter in a saucepan. Blend in flour and cook over low heat until mixture is smooth and bubbly. Remove from heat; stir in salt, pepper, half and half, cayenne and cheese. Return to heat, stirring constantly to make a smooth sauce. Reduce heat and keep warm until sandwiches are assembled. Place 2 slices of toast on each serving plate. Top with meat of your choice and cover with cheese sauce. Mound french fries on top. Serve hot.

Serves 4.

Springfield

Springfield became the capital of Illinois in 1837, nineteen years after statehood was granted. This historic area is rich in reminders of the sixteenth U.S. President, Abraham Lincoln, who lived here for twenty-four years. Among the many noteworthy landmarks is the Lincoln Home National Historic Site. Corn dogs, an Illinois tradition, were invented at Springfield's Cozy Dog Drive-in on Route 66.

Chocolate Lovers' Chili

"Our church had a chili supper and contest. This recipe was my successful experiment."

Betty R. Drapalick—Waukegan

2 cups chopped ONION
2 cloves GARLIC, minced
3 lbs. extra lean GROUND BEEF
2 tsp. SALT
2 cans (6 oz. ea.) TOMATO PASTE
2 cans (15 oz. ea.) DARK RED
    KIDNEY BEANS, undrained

3 Tbsp. CHILI POWDER
1 Tbsp. CUMIN SEED
7 BEEF BOUILLON CUBES
3 cups WATER
1/2 tsp. TABASCO®
1/2 tsp. BLACK PEPPER
1/2 oz. BAKING CHOCOLATE

In a large skillet, add onion, garlic, ground beef and salt; cook until meat is no longer pink. Add tomato paste and kidney beans. Stir well. Add chili powder and cumin seed. In bowl, dissolve beef bouillon cubes in water. Add to beef mixture. Stir well. While stirring, add Tabasco, pepper and chocolate. Cover and simmer for 2 1/2 hours, stirring frequently.

Flemish Cod

Evelyn VanPuyvelde—Moline

4 med. ONIONS, finely chopped
4 COD FILLETS
1 cup ALL-PURPOSE FLOUR
1 Tbsp. BUTTER
4 slices LEMON

4 BAY LEAVES
SALT and PEPPER to taste
1 can (12 oz.) DARK BEER
1/2 cup BREAD CRUMBS

In a skillet, sauté onions until brown; spread in a 9 x 13 buttered ovenproof dish. Dredge fillets in flour; place butter in a skillet and cook fish rapidly on both sides to seal. Arrange fish on top of onions and garnish with additional butter, slices of lemon and bay leaves. Sprinkle with salt and pepper and pour beer around fish. Bake at 350° for 20 minutes. Sprinkle bread crumbs over top 5 minutes before removing from oven. Remove bay leaves before serving.

Midwestern Chili

"Of all our chili recipes, this is our favorite. It was developed by my mother more than 30 years ago."

Frank J. Boblak—Real Estate Counselor, Elk Grove Village

2 lbs. GROUND CHUCK
2 Tbsp. CANOLA OIL
1 lg. ONION, diced
1 sm. GREEN BELL PEPPER, diced
1 clove GARLIC, minced
2 Tbsp. BUTTER
2 cans (10.75 oz. ea.) TOMATO SOUP
2 cans WATER
SALT and PEPPER to taste
1 tsp. PAPRIKA
1/8 tsp. crushed RED PEPPER FLAKES
2 tsp. CHILI POWDER
1 tsp. CUMIN
1 can (15 oz.) DARK RED KIDNEY BEANS

In a large skillet, brown meat in oil. Set aside. In another skillet, sauté onion, green pepper and garlic in butter until onion is translucent. Place meat and vegetables in a Dutch oven. Add soup, water, salt, pepper, paprika and red pepper flakes. Simmer for 4 hours with cover slightly ajar to permit the steam to escape. Add chili powder, cumin and kidney beans. Bring to a boil. Simmer an additional hour.

Serves 4-6.

Evanston

Originally named Grosse Point, this important lake port was renamed in honor of John Evans, one of the founders of Northwestern University. Founded in 1851, Northwestern is one of the nation's leading private universities. Additional institutions of higher learning, the headquarters of Rotary International and the Woman's Christian Temperance Union can also be found here.

Individual Ham Loaves

"My friend, Marge Dimmitt, gave me this recipe. I also make these loaves and then freeze them for later use. Pittsfield hosts the annual Pike County Pig Days celebration which is held the first weekend after the 4th of July."

Glenna Ferguson—Pittsfield

7 1/2 lbs. GROUND PORK	10 cups CRACKER CRUMBS
5 lbs. GROUND HAM	MILK to moisten
10 EGGS	SALT and PEPPER to taste

Combine all ingredients and fill individual loaf pans with about 1/4-pound of meat mixture. Brush tops of loaves with **Brown Sugar Sauce** and bake at 350° for 1/2 hour.

Serves 52.

Brown Sugar Sauce

4 1/2 cups packed BROWN SUGAR	1 1/2 cups VINEGAR
1 1/2 cups WATER	3 tsp. DRY MUSTARD

In a large bowl, combine all ingredients and stir well.

Seven-in-One Dish

"This is an easy to make main dish that smells terrific while cooking!"

Jeanne Plotz—Litchfield

1 lb. HAMBURGER	3 POTATOES, cubed
1 med. ONION, diced	1 can (10.75 oz.) TOMATO SOUP
2 stalks CELERY, diced	1 can (15 oz.) SWEET PEAS
6 CARROTS, sliced	

In a skillet, brown hamburger and sauté onion and celery. Add carrots, potatoes and soup. Cover and cook for 45 minutes. Add peas and cook for an additional 15 minutes or until vegetables are tender.

Autumn's Swiss Supper

"This is a favorite dish for cool fall nights. I like to make it because it is easy (I make it in my crockpot) and because it makes such a delicious family supper!"

Karen Worner—Metamora

1 1/2 lbs. SWISS STEAK, sliced into thin strips
3/4 cup ALL-PURPOSE FLOUR
1 sm. SWEET ONION, thinly sliced
1 sm. GREEN BELL PEPPER, thinly sliced
1/2 lb. fresh MUSHROOMS, sliced
4 med. unpeeled RED POTATOES, thinly sliced
1 1/2 cups BABY CARROTS, halved
1 can (16 oz.) STEWED TOMATOES, sliced
1 tsp. SUGAR
1/2 tsp. PEPPER
1 tsp. WORCESTERSHIRE SAUCE
1 BEEF BOUILLON CUBE
1/2 cup BOILING WATER

Dredge meat thoroughly in flour. Lay strips evenly in a large crockpot or slow cooker. Place onion on meat, then bell pepper, mushrooms, potatoes and carrots. Top with stewed tomatoes; sprinkle with sugar, pepper and Worcestershire sauce. Dissolve beef bouillon in boiling water and add to mixture. Cover and cook on HIGH for 5 hours or LOW for approximately 8 hours. Serve with hot rolls and a tossed salad.

Serves 6.

Peoria

Peoria is home to the world's largest solar system model. Peoria has its own ballet and civic opera company productions as well as the 10th oldest symphony orchestra in the nation. Nestled on the banks of the Illinois River, Peoria is well-known for its riverboat cruises and the Par-A-Dice Riverboat Casino.

Wimpies

"As I was growing up, we especially enjoyed these sandwiches because they included the tomatoes, green peppers and cabbage from our garden."

Marilyn Harres—Columbia

2 lbs. GROUND BEEF
1 cup chopped ONIONS
1 cup chopped CELERY
1/2 cup diced GREEN BELL
    PEPPER
6 TOMATOES, peeled and
    chopped
1 cup PEPSI COLA®
1 cup BROOKS® CATSUP
2 Tbsp. BROWN SUGAR

2 Tbsp. VINEGAR
1 Tbsp. WORCESTERSHIRE
    SAUCE
1/4 tsp. CELERY SEED (optional)
1/4 tsp. SWEET BASIL (optional)
1 can (4 oz.) MUSHROOM
    PIECES
HAMBURGER BUNS
COLE SLAW

In a large skillet, brown ground beef and sauté onions; drain meat drippings. Add celery, bell pepper and tomatoes. In a bowl, combine the next seven ingredients. Add to meat mixture in skillet and cook down, over medium heat, until thick. Just before serving, add mushrooms and heat a few minutes longer. Place meat mixture on bottom half of hamburger buns and top with a serving of *Cole Slaw.*

Cole Slaw

1/2 cup SUGAR
2 tsp. OIL
2 Tbsp. WHITE VINEGAR
SALT and PEPPER to taste

1/2 cup COLD WATER
1 sm. ONION, diced
1/2 head CABBAGE,
    shredded

In a small bowl, combine sugar with oil then add vinegar, salt, pepper, water and onion; mix well. Place cabbage in a bowl; pour mixture over cabbage and toss thoroughly.

Blackened Chicken Quesadillas

"I like to cook anything and everything. There is no particular style or cuisine that I consider my favorite."

Klaudia B. Crawford—Country Cupboard Cafe, Long Grove

1/2 lb. boneless, skinless CHICKEN BREASTS
4 Tbsp. CAJUN SEASONING
3 Tbsp. OLIVE OIL
4 FLOUR TORTILLAS
2 cups shredded CHEDDAR CHEESE
1/2 cup diced GREEN ONIONS
2 cups diced TOMATOES
NONSTICK COOKING SPRAY

In a medium bowl, combine the chicken, seasoning and olive oil and mix well until chicken is well-coated. Heat a heavy-bottomed skillet over high heat for several minutes. Cook the chicken breasts on each side until blackened (not burnt) and cooked through, but still moist. Remove chicken and cool slightly. Dice breasts into cubes about 1/2-inch thick. Fill each tortilla evenly with chicken, cheese, green onions and tomatoes. Fold tortillas over to enclose filling. Spray a large skillet with nonstick cooking spray and heat over medium heat. Cook quesadillas, turning once, until golden brown on each side and the cheese has melted. Remove from pan and cut into wedges. Serve with sour cream and guacamole, if desired.

Serves 4.

Winnetka

A charming village north of Evanston and Chicago, Winnetka is a lovely place to shop and dine. A variety of luxurious quality boutiques, specialty shops and restaurants fill the tree-lined streets.

Goulash

(also known as Gulasch—German stew)

"I am a native German. When I moved to Belleville with my American husband, I was thrilled to find out how much German ancestry there is in the area."

Martina Bias—Belleville

1 lb. STEW MEAT
1 lg. ONION, chopped
1 can (4.5 oz.) MUSHROOMS, drained
1 GREEN BELL PEPPER, cut into strips
3-4 cups WATER
CURRY, PAPRIKA, SALT and PEPPER to taste
2 Tbsp. FLOUR
1 cup SWEET CREAM
KETCHUP to taste

In a skillet, brown meat. Add onion, mushrooms and bell pepper. Cook for 10 minutes; add water and season to taste. Simmer for an hour. In a bowl, mix flour with sweet cream, pour through a strainer and then add to skillet. Boil for 5 minutes. Add ketchup to taste. Serve over noodles, mashed potatoes or rice.

Easy Salmon Patties

"I am a hairdresser and exchange recipes with many of my clients. I love to collect cookbooks!"

Mary Lou Chinn—Belleville

1 can (16 oz.) PINK SALMON
1 1/2 tsp. BAKING POWDER
1 EGG

1/3 cup chopped ONION
1/2 cup FLOUR
SHORTENING for frying

Drain salmon, reserving juice. Add baking powder to 2 tablespoons of juice; set aside. In a bowl, combine salmon, balance of salmon juice, egg and onion. Stir in flour. Combine both mixtures. Form into small patties; fry in shortening until golden brown.

Crabmeat & Artichoke Quiche with Roasted Red Pepper Bernaise

Jonathan M. Winkle—Jonathan's Custom Catering, Elgin

3 BAKING POTATOES
2 Tbsp. OLIVE OIL
1/4 tsp. GARLIC POWDER
8 lg. EGGS
1 Tbsp. HALF and HALF
2 Tbsp. ALL-PURPOSE FLOUR
8 oz. SWISS CHEESE, grated
1 sm. ONION, coarsely chopped
1 can (14 oz.) ARTICHOKE HEARTS*
Dash of BLACK PEPPER
1/8 tsp. NUTMEG
Dash of CELERY SALT
1 can (6 oz.) LUMP CRABMEAT, drained

Slice unpeeled potatoes 1/4-inch thick; sauté in olive oil over medium heat until tender; add garlic. Set aside to cool. When cooled, line a 9-inch pie pan, including the sides, with potatoes. Preheat oven to 350°. Combine eggs, half and half and flour; beat until fluffy. Drain and squeeze liquids from artichoke hearts. In a separate bowl, combine cheese, onion, artichoke hearts, pepper, nutmeg, celery salt and crabmeat; lightly stir; add to potato-lined pie pan. Pour egg mixture over all. Bake for 50 to 60 minutes or until knife inserted in center comes out clean. Serve one tablespoon of *Roasted Red Pepper Bernaise* over each slice of quiche.

Serves 6-8.

*Do not use marinated artichoke hearts for this recipe.

(Continued on next page)

Did You Know?

Both the Chicago Mercantile Exchange and the Chicago Board of Trade provide visitors galleries overlooking their commodities trading floors.

Roasted Red Pepper Bernaise

1 sm. roasted RED PEPPER
1 stick UNSALTED BUTTER, melted
1/4 tsp. fresh LEMON JUICE
Dash of SEASONED SALT
2 lg. EGG YOLKS, room temperature

In a food processor, purée red pepper, melted butter, lemon juice and seasoned salt. In a double boiler, over medium heat, quickly whisk egg yolks; slowly add butter mixture; whisk until thickened. Remove from heat.

Easy Chicken Pot Pie

"This recipe is a family favorite. Whenever I make it there are never any leftovers."

Hope Boston—Elgin

1/4 cup chopped ONION
1/4 cup chopped CELERY
1/4 cup BUTTER
1/3 cup FLOUR
SALT and PEPPER to taste
1 can (14.5 oz.) CHICKEN BROTH
1/2 cup MILK
1 pkg. (10 oz.) frozen PEAS AND CARROTS
2 cups cooked, cubed CHICKEN BREASTS
1 pkg. (10 oz.) refrigerated BISCUITS

In a 4-quart saucepan sauté onion and celery in butter until tender. Add flour, salt and pepper. Cook and stir over low heat until bubbly. Stir in chicken broth and milk. Bring to a boil. Cook and stir until mixture has thickened. Stir in frozen vegetables and chicken. Pour mixture into a 13 x 9 baking pan. Separate dough into 10 biscuits, then split each into 2 halves. Place close together on top of chicken mixture. Cut several slits in biscuit tops. Bake at 375° for 20-25 minutes.

Serves 6.

Side Dishes

Spätzle

(also known as Spaetzle—German noodles)

"My mother-in-law's family emigrated from Germany. I learned to make these noodles by watching her make them."

Phyllis Eggert—Libertyville-Mundelein Historical Society, Libertyville

2 cups FLOUR
3 EGGS
1 tsp. SALT
WATER

1 cup finely ground BREAD CRUMBS
3/4 cup MARGARINE

Combine flour, eggs and salt, adding enough water to make a smooth batter. Bring a large pan of water to a boil. Wet spätzle board with a knife and spread a small amount of the batter on the board. Push batter off with a knife into boiling water. Cook until noodles float (about 5 minutes). Drain and set aside in warm water. In a large skillet, melt margarine; stir in bread crumbs and brown. Fold in drained noodles and serve.

Apple Sweet Potatoes with Raisins & Pecans

"My brother got this recipe for me years ago when he worked as a 'bootlegger' at Circa 21 Dinner Playhouse in Rock Island, Illinois. It's a family favorite I make every Thanksgiving."

Carrie Sanden-Roe—Blue Moon Farm, Coal Valley

2 cans (40 oz. ea.) SWEET
   POTATOES, drained*
2 cups peeled, sliced APPLES
1/2-1 cup seedless RAISINS
3 cups MINIATURE
   MARSHMALLOWS
1 cup SUGAR

1 tsp. SALT
1 tsp. CINNAMON
1/2 cup chopped PECANS
1 Tbsp. CORNSTARCH
1/2 cup WATER
2 Tbsp. MARGARINE OR
   BUTTER

Place sweet potatoes in a buttered 9 x 13 baking dish. Add apples and raisins in layers and top with marshmallows. In a bowl, mix together sugar, salt, cinnamon and pecans. Sprinkle over marshmallows. Mix cornstarch with water until smooth. Pour over all. Dot with margarine and bake at 350° for 60 minutes.

*For better taste and color, use 5 lbs. of fresh sweet potatoes that have been boiled or steamed until tender and then skinned.

Pepper Relish

"We raise many of our vegetables in the summer. This recipe is good to use all year round."

Mrs. Paul H. Brinkmann—Dupo

12 RED BELL PEPPERS
12 GREEN BELL PEPPERS
12 sm. ONIONS

2 cups VINEGAR
2 cups SUGAR
1 1/2 Tbsp. SALT

Wash peppers. Chop peppers and onions and cover with boiling water. Let stand for 5 minutes, drain and repeat. In a saucepan, combine vinegar, sugar and salt; bring mixture to a boil then add pepper and onion mixture. Simmer for 10 minutes. Let cool and then freeze.

Carrot Soufflé

"This is a great way to dress up any vegetable."

Mrs. Virginia Herzog—Bensenville

1 cup FLOUR
2 cups HOT MILK
3 EGGS, separated
1 ONION, diced

4 cups CARROTS, cooked
and mashed
1/2 tsp. SALT

In a bowl, mix flour, hot milk and egg yolks. Add onion, carrots and salt. Beat egg whites and fold into mixture. Pour into a ring mold in a pan of hot water. Bake at 350° for 45 minutes. Turn mold onto serving plate and fill center with creamed peas, chicken or fish.

Mt. Vernon

Mt. Vernon is near Rend Lake and serves as a gateway to this expansive wildlife and recreation area. It is also the site of the largest hospitality complex in Southern Illinois as well as home to a unique motorcycle museum, Wheels Through Time.

Italian Tomato Sauce

"I have been married for 40 years and have used this recipe to make a lot of spaghetti and lasagna for my family."

Maxine Martin—Bonnie

2 ONIONS, chopped
1 GREEN BELL PEPPER,
chopped
1 clove GARLIC, minced
1/4 cup OLIVE OIL
SALT and PEPPER to taste
1 can (4 oz.) TOMATO PASTE

4 cups chopped TOMATOES
1/2 cup WATER
1/2 tsp. THYME
1 tsp. OREGANO
1/2 cup grated PARMESAN
CHEESE

Sauté onion, pepper and garlic in oil until soft. Add remaining ingredients, except cheese. Cook slowly for 1 hour. Add cheese. For a meat sauce, add 1 lb. cooked hamburger.

Old-Fashioned Cranberry-Orange Relish

"This is my mother's recipe. She made it for her family which included 10 children. I make up to 20 batches of this relish each year to give as gifts."

Alice S. Billman—Barrington

3 med. unpeeled JONATHAN APPLES, washed and cored
2 ORANGES, 1 peeled, 1 not peeled
1 lb. CRANBERRIES, washed and drained
1 3/4-2 cups SUGAR

Cut unpeeled apples into small chunks. Cut the oranges into pieces, removing seeds and white membranes. Grind the cranberries, apples, and oranges in a food grinder. Include all the juices in the relish. Add the sugar and mix well. Refrigerate for at least 5 days before serving. It is the "ripening" in your refrigerator which brings out the brilliant color and full flavor of this delicious relish.

Kugelis
(Potato Pudding)

"This is a family recipe brought from Lithuania."

Mrs. J. P. Keserauskis—Fairview Heights

10 med. POTATOES
1/2 cup SOUR CREAM
1 Tbsp. melted BUTTER
1 med. ONION, chopped

4 Tbsp. FARINA, OATMEAL
or BREAD CRUMBS
2 EGGS, beaten
SALT and PEPPER to taste

Peel and grate potatoes. In a bowl, add potatoes and remaining ingredients. Mix well. Pour into a greased 9 x 13 baking dish. Bake at 375° for 1 hour, reduce heat and bake until potatoes are tender.

Corn Casserole

"Somonauk is in the heart of farming community. Corn and soybeans are major commodities produced in this area. This corn casserole reflects a modern version of an old standby."

Madelyn Crouch—Somonauk Business Assn., Somonauk

1 can (15 oz.) CREAM STYLE CORN
1 can (15.25 oz.) WHOLE KERNEL
   CORN
1/2 cup BUTTER
1 cup SOUR CREAM

2 EGGS
1 box JIFFY® CORN
   MUFFIN MIX
1 cup grated CHEDDAR
   CHEESE

Do not drain corn. Mix all ingredients together, except cheese. Pour into a greased 9 x 13 baking pan. Sprinkle cheese over top and bake at 350° for approximately 25 minutes, until set and brown.

Horseradish Ring Mold

Susan Williams—Ingleside

1 pkg. (3 oz.) LEMON JELL-O®
1 cup BOILING WATER
1 tsp. VINEGAR

3/4 tsp. SALT
1 jar (5 oz.) HORSERADISH
1 cup WHIPPED CREAM

Dissolve Jell-O in boiling water; let cool for 10 minutes. Add balance of ingredients; pour into ring mold and refrigerate. Excellent with prime rib or corned beef.

Frozen Sweet Corn

"Illinois grows the best sweet corn! I have used this recipe for years and we enjoy the corn all through the snowy winters."

Bernice Maness—Sycamore

8 cups SWEET CORN KERNELS
1/2 cup WATER
4 Tbsp. BUTTER or MARGARINE

SALT to taste
2 Tbsp. SUGAR

Mix all ingredients in a large saucepan. Bring to a boil over medium heat, stirring often. Boil for 5 minutes, then reduce heat. Cool to lukewarm; pack in plastic freezer bags and freeze.

Cabbage Casserole

"This dish is very popular at our church dinners."

Karen Ann Horton—Belle Rive

1 med. CABBAGE
1 tsp. SALT

1 1/2 cups BREAD CRUMBS
1/2 cup melted MARGARINE

Coarsely chop cabbage; place in a pan of salted water and boil for 8 to 10 minutes; drain. Place half of the boiled cabbage in a buttered 3-quart baking dish. Pour half of the **White Sauce** over the cabbage. Mix bread crumbs and margarine then sprinkle half of this mixture over the sauce. Repeat with remaining cabbage, white sauce and bread crumb mixture. Bake at 350° for 35 minutes.

White Sauce

1/3 cup MARGARINE
4 Tbsp. FLOUR

1 1/2 cups MILK
SALT and PEPPER to taste

Melt margarine in a saucepan. Add flour and slowly stir in milk. Cook and stir until thick. Stir in salt and pepper.

Baked Pumpkin

"We raise pumpkins on the site of what was once the historic town of Dresden. Grandma's house was originally a stagecoach stop, built in 1834. Our barn, called the 'Mule Barn' is in the National Register of Historic Places. Pumpkins are a highly prized vegetable because, when stored in a cool dry place, they can be kept for months."

Noreen Dollinger—Dollinger Family Farm, Minooka

Cut **PUMPKIN** in half, then quarters. Remove seeds. Place in a baking dish with the rind side down. Bake at 350° for appriximately 1 hour or until tender. Scoop out flesh, place in a casserole dish. Dot with butter and sprinkle with cinnamon and brown sugar. Return to oven for 10 minutes.

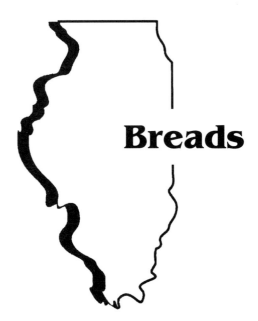

Breads

Sky High Honey Biscuits

"The recipe for these very flaky biscuits came from my mom. The recipe originally called for sugar, but since we have our own beehives, I substituted honey. They turned out even better!"

Kathy Bock—Honey Hill Orchard, Waterman

2 cups WHOLE-WHEAT FLOUR
1 cup ALL-PURPOSE FLOUR
4 1/2 tsp. BAKING POWDER
1/2 tsp. SALT
3/4 tsp. CREAM OF TARTAR
3/4 cup BUTTER or MARGARINE, softened
1 EGG, beaten
1 cup MILK
2 Tbsp. HONEY

Combine dry ingredients. Cut in butter. Add egg, milk and honey. Knead until dough is smooth. Roll out to 1-inch thickness and cut out biscuits with biscuit cutter. Place on a greased cookie sheet. Bake at 450° for 12 to 14 minutes. Serve warm with butter and honey.

Kolac

"My great-grandmother came to America at the age of 13 to marry my great-grandfather, who had just been widowed and had 3 small children who needed a mother. She brought this and many other Slovak recipes with her from the 'Old Country'."

Michelle Schulz—Western Illinois Tourism, Macomb

2 cakes YEAST	1 tsp. SALT
1/2 cup WARM MILK	3 Tbsp. SUGAR
6 cups FLOUR	3 EGGS, beaten
1/2 lb. BUTTER, softened	1 cup SOUR CREAM

Dissolve yeast in warm milk. In a large bowl, combine remaining ingredients. Add yeast and milk mixture. Blend well. Divide dough into four parts and roll out each part into rectangles that are 1/4-inch thick. Spread with **Walnut** or **Poppy Seed Filling.** Roll up, seal ends and place on a greased pan. Brush with melted butter. Pierce tops with tines of a fork and put in a warm place to rise until doubled in size. Bake at 350° for 30 minutes.

Walnut Filling

2 lbs. WALNUTS, ground	2 Tbsp. melted BUTTER
2 cups SUGAR	4 Tbsp. MILK

In a bowl, combine all ingredients.

Poppy Seed Filling

1 lb. POPPY SEEDS	3 Tbsp. MILK
1 cup SUGAR	

In a bowl, combine all ingredients.

The Mississippi—"Old Man River"

The longest river in the U.S., this river has played a vital role in history and remains the nation's chief inland waterway. It borders the entire western boundary of Illinois, finding its widest point at Cairo.

Twister Rolls

"My mother was famous for her yeast breads which she made without written recipes! I helped her figure out the proportions to write this recipe down and entered it in our 4-H contest where it was chosen to go to the State Fair contest."

Phyllis Hepner—Kewanee

2 pkgs. DRY YEAST
1/2 cup LUKEWARM WATER
4 cups MILK
7 Tbsp. MARGARINE
3/4 cup SUGAR

4 tsp. SALT
10 cups FLOUR
MARGARINE, softened
CINNAMON
SUGAR

In a bowl, soften yeast in water. In a saucepan, heat milk and margarine to almost scalding. In a separate bowl, combine sugar and salt. When milk has cooled to lukewarm, add to sugar mixture. Add yeast and stir. Add 5 cups of flour and beat with a mixer until smooth. Stir in the last 5 cups of flour by hand. Dough should be sticky. Grease bottom and sides of a large bowl, add bread dough and grease its top. Cover and put in a warm place to rise until almost double in bulk. Punch down and let rise again. Divide dough into fourths; roll out each portion into a rectangle. Spread with margarine and sprinkle with a mixture of cinnamon and sugar. Roll up each piece of dough and pinch ends to seal. With scissors, snip about 3/4 through rolls at 1-inch intervals. Lift and twist each section to form a ring and place on cookie sheet. Let rise again. Bake at 425° for 10 minutes. Frost with **Powdered Sugar Frosting** and decorate with **MARASCHINO CHERRIES** and **PECAN HALVES**.

Makes 4 rings.

Powdered Sugar Frosting

1 box (1 lb.) POWDERED SUGAR
1/2 cup BUTTER, softened

1 tsp. VANILLA
3 Tbsp. MILK

In a large bowl, beat together the sugar, butter, vanilla and milk until smooth. Add more milk, if needed, until frosting is of spreading consistency.

Braided Egg Bread

"My mother did a lot of baking. She always made these braided loaves for Sundays and for special events."

Arthur J. Holevoet—Atkinson

2 pkgs. ACTIVE DRY YEAST
1/2 cup WARM WATER
1 1/2 cups LUKEWARM MILK
1/4 cup SUGAR
1 Tbsp. SALT
3 EGGS

1/4 cup BUTTER, softened
7 1/4 cups sifted FLOUR
1 EGG YOLK
2 Tbsp. WATER
SESAME SEEDS

In mixing bowl, dissolve yeast in water. Stir in milk, sugar and salt. Add eggs, butter and half of the flour; blend. Add remaining flour and combine. Turn dough onto a lightly floured board. Knead until smooth and blistered, about 5 minutes. Form into a ball and place in a greased bowl; turn ball so greased side is up. Cover with a damp cloth. Let rise in warm place until doubled in bulk, about 1 1/2-2 hours. Punch down; form into a ball and let rise again until almost doubled in bulk, about 30 minutes. Divide dough into 6 parts; form each into a 14-inch long roll. Braid 3 rolls loosely, pinching ends together. Repeat for second braid. Place on 2 greased baking sheets; cover with a damp cloth. Let rise until almost doubled in bulk, 50-60 minutes. Heat oven to 350°. Beat egg yolk and water together. Brush braids with egg yolk mixture and sprinkle with sesame seeds. Bake 30-40 minutes, or until nicely browned.

Rockford

"The Forest City", as nicknamed by its citizens, is the second largest city in Illinois. Bisected by the Rock River, Rockford offers more than 6,000 acres of parks for unlimited outdoor activities including boating, camping and hiking. It has championship golf courses, public gardens, museums and many antique shops, including indoor antique malls.

Southern Illinois Hot Bread

"I've been making this quick and tasty bread for nearly 50 years."

Edna Diefenbach—Harrisburg

1/4 cup MARGARINE, softened	1/2 cup MILK
1 Tbsp. SUGAR	1 cup FLOUR
1 EGG	1 1/2 tsp. BAKING POWDER

In a medium size mixing bowl, cream together margarine and sugar. In another bowl, beat together egg and milk. In a third bowl, combine flour and baking powder and mix well. Alternately combine egg and flour mixtures with butter and sugar mixture, mixing well. Pour into a greased 9-inch pan. Bake at 425° for 20-25 minutes. Cut into squares.

Pumpkin Bread

"Many pumpkins are grown in Illinois, including those in our garden. I often cook fresh pumpkin for this bread."

Kathleen Burris—Opdyke

2/3 cup SHORTENING	1 1/2 tsp. SALT
2 2/3 cups SUGAR	1/2 tsp. BAKING POWDER
4 EGGS	1 tsp. CINNAMON
1 can (16 oz.) PUMPKIN	1 tsp. CLOVES
2/3 cup WATER	2/3 cup chopped NUTS
3 1/3 cups FLOUR	2/3 cup RAISINS
2 tsp. BAKING SODA	

Preheat oven to 350°. Grease 2 (9 x 5) loaf pans. Cream shortening and sugar thoroughly. Add eggs, pumpkin and water. Blend in dry ingredients. Mix well. Stir in nuts and raisins. Pour into greased loaf pans and bake for 65-75 minutes.

Raspberry Mint Muffins

"I grow 625 varieties of herbs and 76 varieties of scented geraniums in my greenhouses. I also teach classes on growing and using herbs."

Wilma Clark—Clark's Greenhouse and Herbal Country, San Jose

2 cups FLOUR
2 tsp. BAKING POWDER
1/2 tsp. SALT
1/2 cup BUTTER, softened
3/4 cup SUGAR
1/2 cup packed BROWN SUGAR
2 EGGS
1 tsp. VANILLA
1/2 cup MILK
2 1/2 cups fresh RASPBERRIES*
1/4 cup finely chopped fresh MINT LEAVES

In a large mixing bowl, combine flour, baking powder and salt; set aside. In an electric mixer bowl, cream the butter. Add both sugars to the butter and cream at high speed. Add eggs, one at a time, creaming after each addition. Add vanilla and beat again. Add half of the milk, then half of the dry ingredients, mixing only enough to moisten the dry ingredients. Add remainder of milk and dry ingredients, again mixing only enough to moisten. Mash 2 cups of the berries and mix them into the batter. Fold in the remaining whole berries and the chopped mint leaves. Grease muffin cups and spoon batter into each until 2/3 full. Bake at 375° for 25 to 35 minutes or until a toothpick inserted into the middle of a muffin comes out clean. Cool for 10 minutes in pan, then remove and serve either hot or cool.

Makes 18 muffins.

*Frozen, thawed and drained berries may be used.

Melt-In-Your-Mouth Pumpkin Bread

"I have made this bread for years for Christmas dinners. It is very moist and keeps for a long time."

Mable R. Markland—Galesburg

1 1/4 cups OIL
5 EGGS
2 cups PUMPKIN
2 cups FLOUR
2 cups SUGAR

2 pkgs. (3 oz. ea.) INSTANT
COCONUT PIE FILLING
1 tsp. SALT
1 tsp. BAKING SODA
1 tsp. CINNAMON

In a bowl, combine oil, eggs and pumpkin thoroughly. In another bowl, combine remaining ingredients and mix well. Combine both mixtures and pour into 2 greased large loaf pans or 6 small ones. Bake for 50 minutes at 375°.

Maple & Brown Sugar Muffins

"I got this recipe from my great-grandmother."

Krista L. Page—Bloomington

1 1/4 cups FLOUR
1 cup MAPLE & BROWN SUGAR
    FLAVORED MALT-O-MEAL®
1/3 cup SUGAR
3/4 cup MILK

1/4 cup VEGETABLE OIL
1 EGG
1 Tbsp. BAKING POWDER
1/2 tsp. SALT
1 Tbsp. VANILLA

Preheat oven to 400°. In a large mixing bowl, combine all ingredients and stir until moistened. Pour into greased muffin cups to 3/4 full. Bake for 18 to 20 minutes or until a toothpick comes out clean.

Makes 12 muffins.

Polish Babka

"This recipe is for a simple yeast bread, or Babka. Babka means grandma in Polish. In other words, it is the kind of bread Grandma used to make, especially around the holidays."

Frank J. Boblak—Elk Grove Village

1/2 cup BUTTER, softened
1/2 cup SUGAR
1 tsp. SALT
1 cup MILK, scalded
5 EGGS, beaten
2 pkgs. DRY YEAST
1/2 cup LUKEWARM WATER
ZEST from 1 LEMON

1 tsp. crushed or powdered
   CARDAMOM SEEDS
5 cups UNBLEACHED FLOUR
1/2 cup blanched and chopped
   ALMONDS (optional)
1 EGG YOLK
2 tsp. WATER
POWDERED SUGAR

In a bowl, add butter, sugar and salt to scalded milk; let cool to lukewarm. Add eggs to milk mixture. Dissolve yeast in lukewarm water. Add yeast mixture, lemon zest and cardamom to milk and egg mixture. Add flour in gradually and beat until smooth; about 10 minutes. Place dough in a well-greased bowl. Place bowl in a warm place. Let rise to double. Punch down. Coat a fluted pan with butter and sprinkle with flour. Place chopped almonds in bottom of pan. Add dough to the pan. Let rise to double. Beat egg yolk and water together and brush on top of dough. Bake at 350° for 30 minutes. Sprinkle the top with powdered sugar.

Did You Know?

Illinois has been growing corn since the pioneer days. Corn thrives on about 40 percent of the state's farmland and accounts for nearly a fifth of the nation's corn crop. Illinois is also a leader in popcorn production. The average American eats about 68 quarts of popped popcorn a year and, as a nation, we consume 17.3 billion quarts annually.

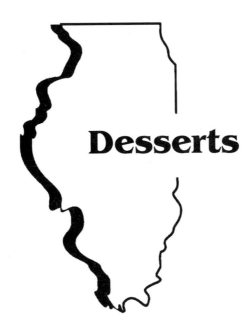

Desserts

Hummingbird Cake

"For 19 years I've made this cake and I still don't understand why it's called 'Hummingbird Cake'! My children love it. Hummingbirds arrive at my home in central Illinois one week before Mother's Day and leave on September 18th—every year!"

Janet D. Hinrichsen—Goodfield

3 cups sifted FLOUR
2 cups SUGAR
1 tsp. BAKING SODA
1 tsp. SALT
1 tsp. CINNAMON
3 EGGS, beaten

1 1/2 cups OIL
1 1/2 tsp. VANILLA
1 can (8 oz.) CRUSHED
    PINEAPPLE and JUICE
2 cups diced BANANAS
1 cup chopped PECANS

In a large bowl, sift dry ingredients. In another bowl, mix eggs and oil. Gently stir into dry ingredients. Add vanilla, pineapple, pineapple juice, bananas and pecans. Stir gently. Bake in a 9 x 13 greased and floured pan at 350° for 50 to 55 minutes. When cake is cool, frost with a thin layer of **POWDERED SUGAR FROSTING** (see page 51).

Almost Eli's Original Plain Cheesecake

"In 1980, Eli's Cheesecake made it's public debut at the first Taste of Chicago Food Festival. Since that date, Eli's Cheesecake has been the number one dessert at the annual food festival, selling over one million slices of cheesecake. Eli's Cheesecake is a symbol of Chicago."

Debbie Littmann—The Eli's Cheesecake Company, Chicago

1 1/2 lbs. CREAM CHEESE, room temperature
1 cup SUGAR
Pinch of SALT
1 Tbsp. FLOUR
2 EGGS
2 EGG YOLKS
3/4 cup SOUR CREAM
1 Tbsp. PURE VANILLA
PREPARED PIE CRUST

Heat oven to 350°. Mix cream cheese, sugar, salt and flour in a large mixer bowl until smooth and lump-free. Add eggs and egg yolks, one at a time, mixing and scraping down sides after each addition. Mix in sour cream and vanilla and mix until well-blended. Pour into a greased 9-inch cheesecake pan, pressed with your favorite crust. Bake on center oven rack until cheesecake just barely jiggles in the center when tapped, about 45 minutes. Cool and refrigerate before releasing from pan.

Joliet

Originally named Juliet for Shakespeare's leading character, Joliet was renamed after it was assumed to have been named after the Canadian explorer Louis Joliet, who had visited the region in 1673. Today, it is a thriving entertainment area in the heart of the Illinois and Michigan Canal National Heritage Corridor, boasting four riverboat casinos as well as the renowned Rialto Square Theater.

Welcome Neighbor Apple Cake

"Growing up, we were known as the family at the end of the street with all the apple trees. My mom would make this cake for old and new neighbors."

Rebecca Wallace—Collinsville

2 cups SUGAR
1 1/2 cups VEGETABLE OIL
1 Tbsp. CINNAMON
2 EGGS

3 cups FLOUR
1 tsp. BAKING SODA
1 cup chopped WALNUTS
3 cups fresh, diced APPLES

In a large bowl, mix sugar, oil, cinnamon and eggs. Add remaining ingredients and mix well. Batter will be stiff. Pour into a greased and floured 9 x 13 baking pan. Bake at 350° for 50-60 minutes.

Easy Layer Bars

"This recipe is quick to prepare. There is no mixing!"

Mrs. Elaine A. Pauesick—Collinsville

1 stick MARGARINE
1 1/2 cups GRAHAM CRACKER CRUMBS
1 cup COCONUT FLAKES
1 cup CHOCOLATE CHIPS
1 cup BUTTERSCOTCH CHIPS
1 cup chopped NUTS
1 can SWEETENED CONDENSED MILK

Melt margarine. Pour into a 9 x 13 pan. Sprinkle cracker crumbs over melted margarine, then sprinkle coconut evenly over crumbs. Top with chocolate chips, butterscotch chips and then nuts. Pour sweetened condensed milk over entire mixture. Bake at 350° for 30 minutes, or until lightly brown on top. When cool, cut into bars.

Peach Cup Pudding

"Southern Illinois orchards produce some of the best peaches in the country."

Edna Diefenbach—Harrisburg

1 can (16 oz.) PEACH HALVES	2 cups soft fine BREAD
2 EGGS	CRUMBS
1/2 cup SUGAR	2 Tbsp. melted BUTTER
1 tsp. CINNAMON	

Drain peaches, reserving 1 cup syrup. Place 6 peach halves cut side up in well-oiled custard cups. In a bowl, beat eggs until light and fluffy. Gradually add sugar, beating constantly. Mix in cinnamon, bread crumbs and butter. Pour mixture over peaches. Bake at 400° for 25 minutes. Serve with hot **Sweet Butter Sauce** poured over top.

Sweet Butter Sauce

1 cup PEACH SYRUP*	1/2 tsp. CINNAMON
1/4 cup packed BROWN SUGAR	2 Tbsp. BUTTER
2 Tbsp. CORNSTARCH	

In a saucepan, combine all ingredients. Heat until thick, stirring constantly.

*If using fresh peaches, substitute 1 cup water for syrup.

Carbondale

Near the beautiful recreational lands of Shawnee National Forest is Carbondale, the home of Southern Illinois University. In addition to popular university-owned buildings there are interesting historical sites, including Woodlawn Cemetery, where Memorial Day can be traced to the first post-Civil War service, held in 1866.

Black Walnut Cake

"This is my husband's favorite cake. When we moved to Illinois we were delighted to see the abundant crop of black walnuts in this area."

Verna M. Prater—Belleville

1 cup BUTTER, softened	1 tsp. BAKING SODA
2 cups SUGAR	1 cup BUTTERMILK
1/2 cup SHORTENING	1 cup COCONUT FLAKES
5 EGGS, separated	1 cup chopped BLACK
2 cups FLOUR	WALNUTS

In a large bowl, cream the first three ingredients together, then add egg yolks, one at a time, beating well after each addition. In a separate bowl, mix flour and baking soda together, then add to butter mixture alternately with the buttermilk. Beat well after each addition. Add coconut and black walnuts and mix well. In a small bowl, beat egg whites until stiff; gently fold into batter. Line the bottoms of 3 (9-inch) cake pans with waxed paper. Pour batter into the pans, dividing evenly. Bake at 325° for 20 minutes or until a toothpick comes out clean. Let cake sit in pans for 10 minutes before removing to cake platter. Frost with ***Cream Cheese Frosting.*** Sprinkle top with additional coconut and black walnuts.

Cream Cheese Frosting

8 oz. CREAM CHEESE, softened	16 oz. POWDERED SUGAR
1 stick BUTTER, softened	1 Tbsp. VANILLA

Combine all ingredients in a bowl and then beat with a mixer until smooth.

Did You Know?

The game of softball was developed as an indoor game in 1887 by George W. Hancock of Chicago. He used a 16-inch ball whose seams were turned to the outside. In 1895, Lewis Rober of Minneapolis adapted the game for outdoor play. Rober used a 12-inch ball that had a cover like a baseball.

Grandma's Sugar Cookies

"My Grandma Schrock has been gone for over 30 years, but I still remember that when we showed up at Grandma's house she would always have bags of her sugar cookies ready to share."

Christine J. Junis—Rock Island

1/2 cup SHORTENING
1/2 cup BUTTER or MARGARINE, softened
1 1/2 cups SUGAR
2 EGGS
4 Tbsp. SOUR CREAM, MILK, or BUTTERMILK
1 tsp. BAKING SODA
3-4 cups FLOUR

In a bowl, cream the shortening, butter and sugar together. Beat in the eggs. Add the sour cream (or milk or buttermilk). Sift the baking soda into the first cup of flour and add to the creamed mixture. Then add remaining flour so that the mixture is firm but not sticky. Drop onto cookie sheet by teaspoonfuls. Flatten with a glass dipped in a **SUGAR** and **CINNAMON** mixture. Bake at 350° for 10-12 minutes, or until golden brown.

Yields 4 dozen.

Nauvoo

"Beautiful place" in Hebrew, Nauvoo was named and settled by Mormon leader Joseph Smith in 1839 but the Mormon community remained for only seven years. Today the Joseph Smith Historic Center features many of the original family properties. Nauvoo is a popular tourist town nestled among local vineyards. A popular local product, Nauvoo blue cheese, has been made here since the mid-19th century. The Nauvoo Cheese Company is now one of the largest producers of blue cheese in the U.S.

Shoo-Fly Pie

"This recipe, which was made famous by the Illinois Amish, is from 'Grandma Yoder's Cookbook, Vol. 1'. Grandma Yoder is Mrs. Elvan (Irene) Yoder who, with her husband and two sons, has owned and operated Rockome Gardens for 41 years. Irene's Gift Shop at Rockome Gardens is Grandma's special domain."

Stacy Earnst—Rockome Gardens, Arcola

Filling:

1 EGG, beaten	1 Tbsp. FLOUR
1/4 cup packed BROWN SUGAR	1/2 cup LIGHT CORN SYRUP
1/2 tsp. BAKING SODA	1 cup WARM WATER
1/8 tsp. CINNAMON	1 (9-inch) PIE SHELL

In a large bowl, mix together all the filling ingredients. Pour into pie shell. Sprinkle ***Topping*** on top of filling and bake at 350° for 1 hour.

Topping:

1/2 cup FLOUR	1/8 tsp. CINNAMON
1/4 cup packed BROWN SUGAR	1/8 tsp. SALT
1/4 tsp. BAKING POWDER	2 Tbsp. CRISCO®

Place all dry ingredients in a bowl. Cut in Crisco until mixture is crumbly.

Champaign-Urbana

The town of Urbana was settled in 1822 and the town of Champaign was established thirty years later—across the street! Today this area, in the heart of the rich Illinois cornbelt, is a mecca of culture and activity, primarily due to the presence of the 125-year-old University of Illinois.

To the south are the Amish communities of Arthur and Arcola, where life goes on unchanged from days past. In Arcola can be found Johnny Gruelle's Raggedy Ann and Andy Museum and Rockome Gardens which features a restaurant with authentic Amish meals and 15 acres of lovely flowers and gardens.

Apfelküchle

(German apple fritters)

"I am a native of Germany and have been sharing my recipes with my new friends and family for many yeares."

Martina Bias—Belleville

1 cup SUGAR
2 tsp. CINNAMON
4 lg. APPLES, peeled and cored
3 Tbsp. RUM or RUM EXTRACT
1 1/4 cups FLOUR
1/2 tsp. BAKING POWDER

1/2 tsp. SALT
2 EGGS, separated
1 1/2 Tbsp. OIL
1/2 cup BEER
1 qt. OIL for deep frying

Mix sugar and cinnamon. Slice apples into 1/2-inch thick slices; sprinkle with half of the cinnamon sugar mixture and drip with rum. Let stand, covered, for 30 minutes. Baste with developing sugar juices. In a bowl, mix flour, baking powder, salt, egg yolks and oil. Continue mixing, adding beer slowly. Beat egg whites until stiff; fold into dough. Heat oil in deep fryer to about 325°. Dip apple slices in dough and then place in oil. When done, drain on paper towels. Sprinkle with remaining cinnamon sugar while still hot.

Jays Potato Chip Cookies

"The founder's wife added potato chips to recipes to stretch meals and to introduce them as a great addition to any recipe."

Carol Ellis—Jays Foods, LLC, Chicago

1 cup BUTTER, softened
1/2 cup SUGAR
1 3/4 cups sifted FLOUR
1/2 cup chopped PECANS

1/2 cup crushed JAYS®
    POTATO CHIPS
1 tsp. VANILLA

In a bowl, cream butter, sugar and flour thoroughly. Add remaining ingredients. Place 1/2 to 3/4 teaspoonfuls of dough on an ungreased cookie sheet about 2 inches apart. Bake at 350° for 10-12 minutes. Cool and sprinkle with powdered sugar.

Makes 6 dozen.

Peach Cobbler

"When I make this peach cobbler it brings family and friends from all over town."

Ingrid Ava Fortinberry—Kankakee

Filling:
    4 cans (16 oz. ea.) sliced PEACHES in heavy syrup
    1 tsp. CINNAMON
    2 tsp. NUTMEG
    1 1/2 tsp. VANILLA
    1 stick BUTTER, cut into pieces
    2 1/2 cups SUGAR
    1/2 tsp. LEMON EXTRACT
    1/2 tsp. BUTTER FLAVOR EXTRACT
    1/2 cup WARM WATER
    4 Tbsp. FLOUR
Crust:
    1 box (2 sheets) pre-made PIE CRUST DOUGH
    1 Tbsp. SUGAR

In a 2-quart saucepan, add 3 cans of peaches and their juice and peaches only from the 4th can. Add the balance of the filling ingredients, except warm water and flour. Cook over a medium heat for 30-35 minutes until peaches are softened slightly; stir occasionally. Divide the pie crust dough and roll out enough to cover the bottom and sides of a 9 x 13 baking pan. Press dough gently into place. Reserve remaining crust for top. Bake crust at 350° until lightly browned. Mix together warm water and flour to a gravy-like consistency. Stir slowly into peach mixture until thickened. Spoon peach mixture into baked crust. Cover cobbler with remaining crust and vent with tines of a fork. Sprinkle sugar over crust and bake at 350° until golden brown and bubbling, about 35-40 minutes.

Kankakee

The Kankakee river runs through this beautiful city which served as a gateway for the first white settlers in the region, leaving behind a rich French heritage.

Cut-Out Cookies

"This has been in my family for 150 years and originated with my great-grandmother Broyhill's family. I remember coming home from school to the wonderful aroma of freshly baked cookies. I could never resist grabbing a few!"

Ellis Wayne Blair—East Peoria

2 cups SUGAR	4 tsp. BAKING POWDER
1 cup BUTTER, softened	1 cup MILK
3 EGGS	1 tsp. VANILLA EXTRACT
6 cups ALL-PURPOSE FLOUR	1 tsp. LEMON EXTRACT

In a large bowl, cream together the sugar and butter. Add eggs and beat until light and fluffy. In a separate bowl, combine flour and baking powder. Add milk and extracts alternately with flour to sugar mixture. Continue adding flour until dough can be formed into a smooth ball. Place dough on a lightly floured pastry board. Roll out to about 1/4-inch thickness. Cut out cookies with a floured cookie cutter and place on ungreased cookie sheets. Bake at 350° for 10-15 minutes or until just done, but not browned.

Buttermilk Pie

"The values and traditions of six nationalities that established themselves in southwest Rockford; Polish, Italian, Lithuanian, African-American, Irish and Hispanic are featured in six separate galleries of our museum. This is an African-American recipe from our files."

Menroy B. Mills—Ethnic Heritage Museum, Rockford

2 cups SUGAR	1 cup shredded COCONUT
5 EGGS	1 tsp. VANILLA
1 stick BUTTER, softened	2 (8-inch) PIE SHELLS
3/4 cup BUTTERMILK	

In a bowl, mix all ingredients together. Divide between pie shells and bake at 350° for one hour.

Caramel Crunch Apple Pie

"This is the best apple pie I have ever tasted. My family enjoys it most when it is still warm and has a scoop of vanilla ice cream on top. I usually make it in the fall when the apples are best."

Joan Holmes—Moline

1 (9-inch) PIE SHELL
24 CARAMELS, unwrapped
3 Tbsp. COLD WATER
4 cups peeled and sliced APPLES
3/4 cup FLOUR

1/3 cup SUGAR
1/2 tsp. GROUND CINNAMON
1/3 cup MARGARINE or
BUTTER, softened
1/2 cup chopped WALNUTS

Preheat oven to 375°. Combine caramels and cold water in a microwavable bowl and heat until melted, about 1-2 minutes. Do not overcook. Spoon apples into unbaked pie shell and drizzle melted caramel mixture over the top. In a bowl, mix flour, sugar and cinnamon. Cut margarine into sugar mixture until mixture resembles coarse crumbs. Stir in walnuts. Sprinkle mixture over top of apples. Bake for 40-45 minutes or until apples are tender.

Strawberry Candy

"This candy is a pretty addition to any Christmas plate."

Mary Redenius—Peoria

2 pkgs. (6 oz. ea.) STRAWBERRY JELL-O®
2 cups POWDERED SUGAR
1 can EAGLE BRAND® SWEETENED CONDENSED MILK
2 cups COCONUT FLAKES
1 cup chopped NUTS
RED SUGAR
SLIVERED ALMONDS, colored green

In a bowl, mix all ingredients together except red sugar and almonds. Create strawberry-size shapes. Roll in red sugar and insert a green almond sliver for a stem.

Hickory Nut Cake

*"This was **the** cake as far as my dad was concerned. He would pick hickory nuts just so my mom would make this cake for him."*

Ellen L. Unger—Charleston

3/4 cup MARGARINE or BUTTER, softened
1 cup SUGAR
1/2 cup packed BROWN SUGAR
3 EGGS, beaten
1 tsp. VANILLA
1 tsp. SALT
3 cups sifted FLOUR
3 tsp. BAKING POWDER
1 cup MILK
1 cup chopped HICKORY NUTS

Cream margarine and sugars together. Add eggs, vanilla and salt; mix gently. Stir in flour, baking powder and milk alternately. Fold in nuts. Pour batter into 2 (9-inch) greased and floured cake pans. Bake at 350° for 40-45 minutes, or until toothpick comes out clean. Top with **POWDERED SUGAR ICING** (see page 51); sprinkle additional nuts over top.

Fresh Strawberry Pie

"This recipe came from my grandmother."

Susan Silberhorn—Susie's Garden Patch, Garden Prairie

1 qt. FRESH STRAWBERRIES
1 box (6 oz.) STRAWBERRY JELL-O®
1/2 cup CORNSTARCH
1 cup WATER
1 (9-inch) BAKED PIE SHELL

Remove stems and divide berries in half. Crush one half of the berries and mix in a saucepan with Jell-O, cornstarch and water. Cook over a low heat until thickened. Cut remaining berries and place one half of them in the bottom of the pie shell. Pour berry sauce over top and layer remaining strawberries over all. Cool. Serve with dollops of whipped cream.

Apple Pudding
with Pudding Sauce

"This recipe comes from my great-grandmother's 'The Home Cookbook of Chicago' that dates back to 1874!"

Marcia Nelson—Marcia's Bed & Breakfast, Ottawa

5 EGGS
1 pint MILK

4 Tbsp. FLOUR
4 APPLES, peeled and grated

In a bowl, mix all ingredients together and pour into a baking dish. Bake at 350° for 75 minutes. Serve with ***Pudding Sauce*** poured over top.

Pudding Sauce

1 cup SUGAR
1/2 cup BUTTER, softened
3 EGG YOLKS

1 tsp. CORNSTARCH
BOILING WATER
WINE or BRANDY to taste

In a bowl, mix sugar, butter, egg yolks and cornstarch until very light. Add enough boiling water to make a thick cream, adding wine or brandy as desired.

Peach Pie

"August is peach time in Southern Illinois! The annual Union County peach harvest is celebrated on the third Friday and Saturday of August at the Cobden Peach Festival."

Carol Hoffman—Southernmost Illinois Tourism Bureau, Ullin

3/4 cup SUGAR
3 Tbsp. FLOUR
1/4 tsp. NUTMEG
Dash of SALT

4 cups sliced fresh PEACHES
2 deep-dish PIE SHELLS
2 Tbsp. BUTTER, softened
1/2 tsp. ORANGE ZEST

Preheat oven to 400°. In a bowl, combine sugar, flour, nutmeg and salt. Fold in peaches. Pour mixture into one pie shell; dot top with butter and sprinkle with orange zest. Top with second pie shell; flute edges and pierce top with tines of a fork. Place pie on a cookie sheet and bake for 40-45 minutes, or until lightly browned.

Royal Chocolate Pie

"I won 5th place with this recipe in the 1991 Illinois State Fair bake-off."

Jeanette Zinck—Nashville

Pie Crust:
   1 1/2 cups sifted FLOUR
   1/2 cup SHORTENING
   1 EGG, beaten
   1/2 tsp. VINEGAR
   2 Tbsp. COLD WATER

Cut shortening into flour until crumbly. In a separate bowl, combine egg, vinegar and water. Add to flour mixture, stirring lightly with a fork until well-blended. Roll out onto lightly floured surface. Place in a 9-inch pie pan. Pour **Chocolate Filling** into pie shell and bake at 350° for 45-50 minutes. Cool. Top with whipped cream or ice cream, as desired.

Chocolate Filling

2 EGGS, well-beaten
2 Tbsp. melted BUTTER
1/2 cup LIGHT CORN SYRUP
1/2 cup packed BROWN SUGAR
1/2 cup PECANS
1/2 cup COCONUT FLAKES
1/2 cup CHOCOLATE CHIPS
1 tsp. VANILLA

Combine all ingredients, mixing well.

Oatmeal Apple Crisp

"This is an easy recipe to make. It is our favorite apple dessert."

Kathy Bock—Honey Hill Orchard, Waterman

5 cups peeled, sliced APPLES
1/2 cup BUTTER, softened
1 1/2 cups ROLLED OATS
1/2 cup packed BROWN SUGAR
1/3 cup FLOUR
1/3 cup chopped PECANS

Place apples in a 2-quart casserole dish. In a bowl, combine remaining ingredients then spread over top of apples. Bake at 350° for 1 hour.

Date Pudding

"This is an old recipe that came from my dad's mother, and possibly from her mother."

Verna M. Prater—Belleville

1/2 stick BUTTER
1 cup packed LIGHT BROWN
  SUGAR
2 cups BOILING WATER
1/2 cup SUGAR
1 cup FLOUR

2 tsp. BAKING POWDER
2/3 cup MILK
1 tsp. VANILLA
1 cup chopped DATES
1/2 cup chopped PECANS

In the bottom of a 9 x 13 baking dish, place butter and brown sugar. Add boiling water and stir to dissolve sugar and melt butter. In a large bowl, mix together the remaining seven ingredients. Drop mixture by spoonfuls to layer evenly over sugar mixture in baking dish. Do not stir. Bake at 375° for 20-30 minutes. Serve warm or cold with **WHIPPED CREAM.**

Holiday Cherry Dessert

"This is a family favorite at many holiday dinners."

Marilyn Harres—Columbia

1 can (14.5 oz.) pitted SOUR CHERRIES, undrained
2/3 cup SUGAR
1/4 tsp. CINNAMON (optional)
1 box (3 oz.) CHERRY GELATIN
1 can (20 oz.) unsweetened CRUSHED PINEAPPLE, drained
1 cup chopped PECANS
WHIPPED CREAM

In a saucepan combine cherries, their juice, sugar and cinnamon; bring to a boil. Remove from heat and add the cherry gelatin mix. Stir until dissolved. Pour mixture into a 9 x 13 glass dish. Add drained pineapple; stir. Sprinkle pecans over the top. Chill until firm and slice into squares to serve. Serve with a dollop of whipped cream on top.

Banana Split Pie Delight

"This is a great treat for summertime get-togethers."

Patty Peek—Leu Civic Center, Inc., Mascoutah

1 box (12 oz.) VANILLA WAFERS, crushed
3/4 cup melted BUTTER
2 cups POWDERED SUGAR
1 cup BUTTER, softened
2 EGGS
5 BANANAS, sliced
1 can (20 oz.) CRUSHED PINEAPPLE, drained
1-2 drops MINT EXTRACT (optional)
1 ctn. (13 oz.) COOL WHIP®, thawed
1 cup chopped NUTS
CHERRY or STRAWBERRY HALVES
ALMOND SLIVERS
CHOCOLATE SYRUP

Combine wafers and melted butter; mix well and press into the bottom of a 9 x 13 pan. In a bowl, combine sugar, butter and eggs. Beat on high speed for 15 minutes. Do not underbeat. Spread mixture on top of wafer crust; top with bananas, then pineapple. Add mint extract to Cool Whip if desired, spread over fruit and sprinkle top with nuts. Garnish with cherries or strawberries, almonds and chocolate syrup, as desired. Chill for at least 4 hours. Cut into squares to serve.

Leu Civic Center

The Leu Civic Center is a United Way Agency serving Scott Air Force Base as well as the surrounding communities. The center offers a variety of youth and family programs including a "Cooking With Kids" class.

Chocolate Zucchini Cake

Diane Zelinske—O'Fallon

1/2 cup BUTTER, softened
1/2 cup VEGETABLE OIL
1 3/4 cup SUGAR
3 EGGS
2 1/2 cups FLOUR
1/4 cup COCOA
1/2 cup SOUR MILK
1 tsp. BAKING SODA
1/2 tsp. BAKING POWDER

1/2 tsp. SALT
1/2 tsp. GROUND CINNAMON
1 tsp. VANILLA
2 cups shredded unpeeled
    ZUCCHINI
1/4 cup packed BROWN SUGAR
1/4 cup chopped WALNUTS
1/2 cup SEMI-SWEET
    CHOCOLATE CHIPS

In a large bowl, combine butter and oil. Add sugar and eggs and cream mixture until smooth. Beat in flour, cocoa and sour milk. Add baking soda, baking powder, salt, cinnamon and vanilla. Combine thoroughly. Stir in zucchini. Pour batter into a 9 x 13 baking pan. Combine brown sugar, walnuts and chocolate chips and sprinkle on top of batter. Bake at 350° for 40 minutes. Cool in pan on rack.

Note: To make sour milk, add 1 tsp. vinegar to 1/2 cup milk.

Coconut Cream Pie

"I got this recipe from my neighbor years ago. It's delicious!"

Mary Ellen Johnson—Mt. Vernon

2 1/4 cups SUGAR
3/4 cup CORNSTARCH
1 tsp. VANILLA
1 tsp. SALT
6 EGGS, separated

5 cups MILK
1 stick MARGARINE
COCONUT FLAKES
2 BAKED PIE SHELLS
1/2 tsp. CREAM OF TARTAR

In a bowl, mix 2 cups sugar, cornstarch, vanilla, salt, egg yolks and 1/2 cup milk. Mix well. In a saucepan, heat remaining milk and the margarine to a boil. Add sugar mixture to milk and cook until thick. Sprinkle coconut on the bottom of pie shells. Add heated mixture, dividing evenly. In a small bowl, beat egg whites with 1/4 cup sugar and cream of tartar until it peaks. Pour over pies. Sprinkle with additional coconut. Bake at 300° for 15 minutes or until pie tops are brown.

White Pie

"This recipe started with my aunt's mother and has been passed down to all of us girls. It is made every Thanksgiving and Christmas and is the first pie to be eaten."

Suzanne Shields—Bluford

3/4 cup SUGAR
1/2 cup FLOUR, less 2 Tbsp.
2 Tbsp. CORNSTARCH
Dash of SALT
2 cups MILK
1 tsp. VANILLA

2 EGG WHITES
1/4 cup SUGAR
1 (9-inch) BAKED PIE SHELL
1 1/2 pints WHIPPING CREAM
Finely chopped NUTS

In a saucepan, mix together the sugar, flour, cornstarch, salt, milk and vanilla. Cook slowly over medium heat, stirring constantly, until mixture has thickened; set aside. Beat egg whites and sugar together to form stiff peaks. Fold into sugar mixture. Pour all into the baked pie shell. Set aside. Whip cream to stiff peaks. Spread on top of pie and sprinkle top with nuts. Refrigerate until ready to serve.

Chinese New Year's Cookies

"Every year just before Christmas our neighborhood has a cookie exchange. I make these quick and easy cookies for that event."

Carroll Flood—Wildwood

1 pkg. (6 oz.) CHOCOLATE CHIPS
1 pkg. (6 oz.) CARAMEL PIECES
1 pkg. (3 oz.) CHINESE NOODLES
1 can SALTED PEANUTS

Melt chocolate chips and caramel pieces in a double boiler. Stir in noodles and peanuts. Drop by teaspoonfuls onto wax paper. Cool.

Makes 3 dozen cookies.

Oatmeal Cookies

"This is an old favorite family recipe. It was given to my mother by Grandma Scott and was my grandfather's favorite cookie."

Marilyn Lila Thomson—Hillsboro

1 cup FLOUR	1 Tbsp. WATER
1/2 tsp. BAKING POWDER	1 tsp. VANILLA
1/2 tsp. BAKING SODA	1 1/2 cups ROLLED OATS
Pinch of SALT	3/4 cup chopped PECANS
1/2 cup SUGAR	3/4 cup RAISINS
1/2 cup packed BROWN SUGAR	3/4 cup COCONUT FLAKES,
1/2 cup SHORTENING	toasted
1 EGG	

In a bowl, sift together flour, baking powder, baking soda and salt. In a separate bowl, cream sugars, shortening, egg, water and vanilla. Add in dry ingredients and beat until smooth. Fold in oats, nuts, raisins and coconut. Shape into 1 1/2-inch balls and place on a cookie sheet. Press down with a glass or tin measuring cup rubbed with shortening and dipped in sugar. Bake at 350° for 12-15 minutes, or until light brown.

Carrot Cookies

Mary Lou Chinn—Belleville

1 cup MARGARINE, softened	1 tsp. VANILLA
3/4 cup SUGAR	2 cups FLOUR
1 EGG	2 tsp. BAKING POWDER
1 cup cooked mashed CARROTS	Dash of SALT

Cream margarine and sugar; add egg, carrots and vanilla and mix well. Add remaining ingredients. Drop dough from a spoon onto an ungreased cookie sheet. Bake at 350° for 15 minutes. Frost with *Orange Frosting.*

Orange Frosting

1 1/2 cups POWDERED SUGAR	1 Tbsp. melted BUTTER
1 tsp. ORANGE ZEST	ORANGE JUICE

Combine sugar, zest and butter and enough orange juice to make frosting of spreading consistency.

Raisin Dumplings

"My mother made these dumplings for as long as I can remember. With seven children it was a very affordable dessert. The aroma while cooking is unbelievably mouth-watering."

Joyce Miesse—The Village Inn Bed & Breakfast, Arthur

Sauce:

1 1/2 cups packed BROWN SUGAR	1 tsp. CINNAMON
2 cups WATER	1/2 tsp. SALT
2 Tbsp. BUTTER	1/2 cup RAISINS

Mix all ingredients in a large saucepan and cook for 5 minutes at a low boil.

Dumplings:
    2 Tbsp. SUGAR
    2 cups BISQUICK®
    3/4 cup MILK

In a bowl, mix all ingredients together and spoon on top of sauce. Cover and simmer for 15 minutes.

Ranger Cookies

"I am 12 years-old and the fourth generation in our family to bake these cookies."

Courtney Brinkmann—Dupo

1 cup BUTTER, softened	1 tsp. BAKING SODA
1 cup SUGAR	1/2 tsp. BAKING POWDER
1 cup packed BROWN SUGAR	1 cup OATMEAL
2 EGGS, beaten	1 cup CORN FLAKES
1 tsp. VANILLA	2 cups RICE KRISPIES®
2 cups FLOUR	

Cream butter and both sugars together, add eggs and vanilla. Stir in remaining ingredients. Drop from a tablespoon onto an ungreased cookie sheet and bake at 350° for 10 minutes.

Makes about 48 cookies.

White Chocolate Cheesecake with Pecan Streusel Swirl

"I developed this recipe at the Pump Room in Chicago where I was the pastry chef. Now I am the executive chef for the Apple Haus here in Long Grove where we make the delicious 3-inch high Uncle Johnny's Brown Bag Apple Pie. I cannot give you that recipe, of course, but know you will enjoy my cheesecake."

J. Carmen Villegas, Executive Chef—Long Grove Apple Haus, Long Grove

Crust:
>2 oz. melted BUTTER
>3 cups finely broken OREO® COOKIES

Preheat oven to 300°. Place 2 (12-inch) sheets of aluminum foil on a counter. Place a springform pan in the middle of each piece of foil. Fold up edges onto sides of springform pan. Mix butter with broken cookies. Divide in half and press to cover bottom of each pan.

Pecan Streusel:

4 oz. finely chopped PECANS	2 Tbsp. CINNAMON
4 oz. ALL-PURPOSE FLOUR	4 oz. BUTTER, softened
4 oz. SUGAR	

Mix all ingredients together in a bowl. Mix only until crumbly. Do not overmix. Set aside.

Cheesecake:

3 lbs. CREAM CHEESE, softened	5 oz. BUTTERMILK
8 oz. SUGAR	1 Tbsp. VANILLA EXTRACT
6 EGGS	3 oz. RUM or BRANDY
10 oz. WHITE CHOCOLATE	

Combine cream cheese and granulated sugar with a paddle mixer until there are no lumps. Be sure to scrape the sides

(Continued next page)

White Chocolate Cheesecake with Pecan Streusel Swirl (Continued)

often. Add eggs, one by one and continue mixing, until mixed thoroughly. Using a double boiler, melt together white chocolate, buttermilk, vanilla and rum or brandy. Pour through a fine strainer. Slowly add to cream cheese and egg mix. Make sure you have a very smooth mixture. Pour in the two prepared springform pans. Add a cup of streusel to each pan and swirl. Do not overswirl or you will lose the effect. Fill a sheet pan with one inch of water. Gently place the two springform pans in the pan. The water is to keep the cheesecake from drying out. Bake at 300° for 50-60 minutes. Garnish with **FRESH RASPBERRIES and RASPBERRY PURÉE SAUCE.**

Did You Know?

In 1837, John Deere, a pioneer blacksmith, developed the first commercially successful, self-cleaning steel plow and in Moline in 1868, Deere & Company was incorporated. Production of John Deere tractors was started in 1918.

Rhubarb Cream Pie

"When we were visiting relatives in Germany last year, they asked me to make an 'American Meal'. The rhubarb plants were beautiful there, so I chose this pie as the dessert."

Jeanne Rehling—Taylorville

1 1/4 cups SUGAR
1/3 cup plus 1 Tbsp. FLOUR
1 cup HALF and HALF
1/2 tsp. CINNAMON
1 (9-inch) PIE SHELL
2 1/2 cups RHUBARB, finely cut

Mix sugar, flour, half and half and cinnamon together. Pour into pie shell. Spread rhubarb over top. Bake for 30 minutes at 400°. Reduce heat to 350° and bake for 30 minutes longer, or until pie sets like custard. Cool before cutting.

Mom's Apple Dumplings

"We make Mom's apple dumplings for special events at our farm, such as the 'Holiday Harvest', an event to benefit the needy children in the area."

Shirley Mills—Mills Apple Farm, Marine

Dumplings:

PASTRY for 2 pie crusts
6 tart APPLES
1/2 cup SUGAR
1/2 tsp. CINNAMON
2 Tbsp. BUTTER, melted

Sauce:

1 cup SWEET APPLE CIDER
1/2 cup SUGAR
1/2 tsp. CINNAMON
3 Tbsp. BUTTER

Roll out pastry into a 1/4-inch thick rectangle and cut into 6-inch squares. Peel and core apples, leaving them whole. Place one apple in the center of each of the pie crust squares. Combine sugar, cinnamon and melted butter and fill centers of apples. Moisten edges of pastry; bring all four corners to the top and pinch to seal; place in a greased baking dish. Bake at 450° for 10 minutes, then at 350° for 30 minutes. Place all sauce ingredients in a saucepan and bring to a boil; simmer until thickened, about 5 minutes. Pour over baked dumplings in serving dishes and serve warm.

Red Raspberry Tapioca

"During most of the summer and up until frost in the fall, we have an abundance of Heritage Red Raspberries."

Phyllis Hepner—Kewanee

1 pkg. (6 oz.) RED RASPBERRY JELL-O®
2 pkgs. (3 oz. ea.) JELL-O® TAPIOCA PUDDING MIX
3 cups BOILING WATER
3 or 4 cups RED RASPBERRIES
1 ctn. (9 oz.) COOL WHIP®

Place gelatin and pudding mix in a bowl; add boiling water and stir to dissolve. Cool. Add berries and stir. Refrigerate until mixture is slightly firm; add Cool Whip and stir again until well-mixed. Refrigerate until ready to serve.

Strawberry Cake

"This is my daughter's favorite birthday cake."

Barbara Parker—Victorian Inn Bed & Breakfast, Rock Island

1 pkg. WHITE CAKE MIX
1 pkg. (4 oz.) STRAWBERRY JELL-O®
4 EGGS
1 cup SALAD OIL
1/2 cup WATER
3 Tbsp. FLOUR
1/2 cup sliced FROZEN STRAWBERRIES, thawed and mashed

Preheat oven to 350°. Grease and flour two (9-inch) round cake pans. Combine first six ingredients and blend well. Fold in the strawberries. Pour batter into cake pans and bake for 30 to 40 minutes. Cool completely then frost with ***Strawberry Frosting.***

Strawberry Frosting

1 box (1 lb.) POWDERED SUGAR
1 stick MARGARINE, softened
1/2 cup sliced FROZEN STRAWBERRIES, thawed and mashed

Combine ingredients and beat until fluffy.

Galesburg

Birthplace of renowned poet, Carl Sandburg, Galesburg lies in the center of the Western River Country. This fertile plain stretches between the Illinois and Mississippi Rivers. Rich in history, Galesburg is remembered as the site of one of the Lincoln-Douglas debates about slavery as well as for its involvement in the Underground Railroad.

Raspberry Cobbler

"This is an old family recipe that is much requested. We also make peach cobbler with it."

Marcia DuPont—Quincy

2-3 pts. fresh RASPBERRIES	1 cup SUGAR
1/4 tsp. ALMOND EXTRACT	1 cup FLOUR
1 EGG	1 tsp. BAKING POWDER
1/4 lb. BUTTER, softened	Dash of SALT

Preheat oven to 350°. Wash and drain raspberries and place in a lightly buttered 9-inch square baking dish. Sprinkle with almond extract. In a medium size bowl, blend egg, butter and sugar. Add flour, baking powder and salt and blend well. Spread egg mixture over top of raspberries and bake for 50 minutes or until top is golden brown. Serve warm with a dollop of whipped cream or a scoop of ice cream.

Kisses

"This recipe dates back to the late 1930s. I haven't found anyone who doesn't like this treat!"

Sharlene Brand—Galesburg

2 EGG WHITES	1 pkg. (6 oz.) CHOCOLATE
1/4 tsp. CREAM OF TARTAR	CHIPS
1/4 tsp. SALT	1/2 cup chopped NUTS
3/4 cup SUGAR	

Combine egg whites, cream of tartar and salt. Beat until stiff but not dry. Add sugar, 3 tablespoons at a time, beating after each addition. Beat until whites stand in peaks. Fold in chips and nuts. Cover cookie sheets with brown paper. Drop batter onto cookie sheets by heaping tablespoons, bringing each to a peak. Bake at 325° for 20 to 25 minutes.

Makes 2 dozen.

Sandy's Cheesecake

"This was my mother's recipe. It is very rich, but also very good! We dress it up with fresh fruit or top it with our favorite, a blueberry sauce."

Sandy Dunphy—The Barn Bed & Breakfast, Dahinda

Crust:
- 15 GRAHAM CRACKERS, crushed
- 1/3 cup melted BUTTER

Filling:
- 4 EGGS
- 1 cup SUGAR
- 24 oz. CREAM CHEESE, softened
- 1 tsp. VANILLA

Topping:
- 1 pint SOUR CREAM
- 3-4 Tbsp. SUGAR
- 1 tsp. VANILLA

Combine graham crackers with butter; spread and press on the bottom of a springform pan. Blend eggs and 1 cup of sugar together until mixture is very thin. Add cream cheese gradually and then vanilla. Beat for 20 minutes. Pour mixture over the graham cracker crust and bake in a 350° oven for 10 minutes. Increase heat to 425° and bake an additional 10 minutes. Remove from oven and cool for 20 minutes. Combine topping ingredients. Add topping to cake and return to 425° oven for 6 minutes. Allow cake to cool for one full hour before placing in refrigerator. Refrigerate 12 hours or overnight before cutting.

Galena

Set in the rugged hills of northwestern Illinois, Galena was a mining and steamboating boomtown in the 1850s and was the home of Ulysses S. Grant. Today it remains a beautifully preserved historic town with some of the finest period architecture in the Midwest.

German Spice Nuggets

"This family favorite has been handed down through several generations."

Marian K. Plass—Villa Park

1 cup DARK CORN SYRUP	1/2 tsp. CINNAMON
1 stick BUTTER	Scant 1/2 tsp. ALLSPICE
1 cup packed DARK BROWN	Scant 1/2 tsp. CLOVES
SUGAR	1/2 tsp. BAKING SODA
1 tsp. SALT	3 or more cups FLOUR

In a 3-quart saucepan, heat the syrup, butter and brown sugar to boiling. Cool to lukewarm. Stir in the salt and spices. Dissolve the baking soda in a little warm water and add to syrup mixture. Transfer mixture to a large bowl. Mix in two cups of flour. Knead in one or more additional cups of flour until the dough is very solid and no longer sticky. Chill the dough. When ready to bake, take a handful of dough and roll into a rope about 3/8-inch in diameter. Slice diagonally into 3/4-inch pieces. Bake on a lightly greased cookie sheet in a 375° oven for 8 minutes. Leave on cookie sheet until cold. (The cookies will come off pan easily and have shiny undersides.) When cool, store in a covered metal container.

Apple Brown Betty

Kathy Bock—Honey Hill Orchard, Waterman

2 cups BREAD CRUMBS	1 tsp. CINNAMON
1/2 cup melted BUTTER	6 cups peeled sliced APPLES
or MARGARINE	1/4 cup WATER
1/2 cup SUGAR	1 Tbsp. LEMON JUICE

Toss bread crumbs with butter. Mix sugar and cinnamon. Add apples and stir until coated. Spread 1/3 crumb mixture in buttered casserole dish. Top with half of the apple mixture. Cover with 1/3 crumbs and remaining apples. Combine water and lemon juice. Pour over apples and top with remaining crumb mixture. Bake, covered, at 375° for 30 minutes. Uncover and bake another 30 minutes. Serve warm with ice cream.

Poverty Cake

"My husband's grandmother didn't have many material things but she was an excellent cook! This is one of her recipes."

Sally Bailey—Springfield

1/2 cup BUTTER, softened
3/4 cup SUGAR
1 EGG
1/2 cup MILK
3/4 cup RAISINS
1/3 cup MOLASSES

2 cups FLOUR
1/2 tsp. BAKING SODA
1/2 tsp. CINNAMON
1/2 tsp. CLOVES
1/2 tsp. NUTMEG

Cream butter and sugar until light. Add egg, milk, raisins and molasses and mix well. Sift flour, mix with balance of ingredients and then combine with butter mixture. Beat very thoroughly (batter will be thin). Pour into an 8 x 8 baking pan and bake for 1 hour at 350°.

Did You Know?

The Quad Cities; Bettendorf and Davenport, Iowa, and Moline and Rock Island, Illinois, combine to create a commercial and manufacturing complex on the Mississippi river in northwestern Illinois.

Oatmeal Fudge Balls

"This was my German grandmother's recipe."

Susan Williams—Ingleside

1 cup SUGAR
3/4 cup SHORTENING
2 squares UNSWEETENED
    CHOCOLATE
1/4 cup COLD COFFEE

1 1/2 cups FLOUR
1/2 tsp. SALT
1/2 cup uncooked OATMEAL
Chopped NUTS

Cream sugar, shortening, chocolate and coffee together. Add flour, salt and oatmeal. Form dough into small balls and then roll in chopped nuts. Bake for 15 minutes at 350°.

Oliebollen

(Dutch for a ball of yeast dough that is deep-fried)

"My great-grandmother in the Netherlands would make these on a wood stove in an iron kettle on New Year's Eve. For 25 years, we have served them at our Dutch Days Celebration here in Fulton. The Celebration is held on the first weekend in May."

Patty Ritzema—Fulton

2 pkgs. YEAST	8 cups FLOUR
1 1/2 cups WARM WATER	6 level tsp. SALT
1 tsp. SUGAR	2 tsp. LEMON ZEST
6 EGGS, well-beaten	2 APPLES, peeled and
2 pints WARM MILK	finely chopped
6 Tbsp. LIGHT CORN SYRUP	POWDERED SUGAR
2 lbs. RAISINS	COOKING OIL

Combine the first 4 ingredients and let stand for 5 minutes. In a large bowl, combine the balance of ingredients except powdered sugar and oil. Add the yeast mixture. Let dough rise until double in size. In a 10-inch kettle, add oil to about 4 inches in depth. Dip 2 tablespoons (approximately 1/8 cup) of batter and drop carefully into hot oil. Batter will form into a ball about the size of a tennis ball. Drain balls on paper towels and then roll in powdered sugar.

Makes 70-80 balls.

The Great River Road

The Great River Road, which extends the length of Illinois from East Dubuque and Galena to Cairo, is a segment of 3,000 miles of highways from the Mississippi's source in Northern Minnesota to the Gulf of Mexico. There are many informational kiosks along the way. Maps and audio cassettes telling you of history, lore and attractions along the Road are available from the Western Illinois Tourism Development Office. Call toll-free (877) GRR-7007.

Mama's Pustkowie

(A bismarck made with yeast)

"My parents came to Illinois around 1915 from Poland. This treat was always made on the Tuesday before Ash Wednesday ('Punchky Day'). I still make them for that day."

Bernadette Anielak—Woodlawn

1 1/3 cups milk	1 tsp. SALT
2 cakes YEAST	2/3 cup melted BUTTER
5 1/2 cups ALL-PURPOSE FLOUR	1 tsp. VANILLA
2 EGGS	1/4 cup RUM
2 EGG YOLKS	1 can (12 oz.) PRUNE or
1 cup SUGAR	APRICOT FILLING

Scald milk and then cool to lukewarm; add yeast. Add half of the flour and mix well. Beat eggs and egg yolks with sugar and salt; add to milk mixture. Add butter, vanilla and rum. Knead in remaining flour. Cover and allow dough to rise in a warm place until spongy, about 2 hours. Place dough on a floured surface and roll out to 1/2-inch thickness. Cut out circles (about 2-inch) with a juice glass. Spread dough apart and insert 2-3 teaspoonfuls filling; press to seal. Allow bismarcks to rise in a warm place until doubled in bulk. Fry in hot, deep fat until brown. Turn once. Drain on absorbent paper. While still warm, sprinkle with **POWDERED SUGAR.**

Billy Sunday Pudding

"This is a Quaker recipe that came from my husband's aunt."

Delores A. Miller—Pawnee

1 cup PEARL TAPIOCA	1 cup chopped NUTS
6 cups WATER	2 cups packed BROWN
1 lb. DATES, chopped	SUGAR

Soak tapioca in water overnight. Add remaining ingredients and stir well. Place in a large baking dish and bake at 350° until tapioca is tender. Serve hot or cold, with cream or whipped topping.

Grandma's Molasses Cookies

"I enjoy baking old family recipes. This one is from my maternal grandmother."

Karen Ann Horton—Belle Rive

2 1/2 cups FLOUR	1/2 cup SUGAR
1/2 tsp. GINGER	1/2 cup MOLASSES
1 tsp. CINNAMON	1 EGG
1/2 tsp. NUTMEG	1/2 cup BUTTERMILK
1 tsp. BAKING SODA	1 cup RAISINS
2/3 cup SHORTENING	1/2 cup chopped NUTS

Sift together the first 5 ingredients. In a large mixer bowl, combine shortening, sugar, molasses and egg. Beat together at medium speed for 2-3 minutes. Add flour mixture and buttermilk alternately and mix on low speed until well-blended. Fold in raisins and nuts. Drop by tablespoons onto a greased cookie sheet and bake for 12 minutes in a 350° oven.

"Life's Recipe"

1 cup GOOD THOUGHTS
1 cup KIND DEEDS
1 cup CONSIDERATION FOR OTHERS
2 cups SACRIFICE FOR OTHERS
2 cups FORGIVENESS
2 cups WELL-BEATEN FAULTS

Mix all together thoroughly with tears of joy, sorrow and sympathy for others. Flavor it with gifts of love. Fold in 4 cups of prayer and faith to lighten the other ingredients.

Joan M. Hickman—Washington

Fairs & Festivals

April—Dutch Days Festival, Fulton
May—Springfest, Amboy
May—Strawberry Spring Festival, Carlinville
May—Springfest, Maeystown
May—St. Patrick Parish Strawberry
    Festival, Ruma
May—Herrinfesta Italiana, Herrin
June—Quig's Father's Day Buffet,
    Mundelein
June—Annual Strawberry Fest, Long Grove
June—Music Festival, Rockford
June—Strawberry Festival, Garden Prairie
June—Strawberry Festival, Catlin
June—Strawberry Festival, Elmwood
June—Turkey Festival, Tremont
June—Strawberry Fest, Newton
June—International Horseradish Festival,
    Collinsville
June—Schweizerfest, Highland
July—Brookfest, Brookfield
July—Puerto Rican Heritage Fest, Aurora
July—Corn Boil Festival, Sugar Grove
July—Chili Cook Off, Batavia
July—German Valley Days, German Valley
July—Scottish Highland Games, Rockford
July—Walleye Festival, Findlay
July—Das Strasburg Festival, Strasburg
July—Sweet Corn Festival, Chatham
July—Bagelfest, Mattoon
July—Pike County Pig Days, Pittsfield
Aug.—Festa Italiana, Rockford
Aug.—Polish Fest, Rockford
Aug.—Annual Porkfest Celebration, Utica
Aug.—Corn Festival, DeKalb
Aug..—Apple Dumpling Festival, Atwood
Aug.—Sweet Corn & Watermelon Fest,
    Mt. Vernon

Aug.—Chili Fest & Corn Boil, Chillicothe
Aug.—Sweet Corn Festival, Urbana
Aug.—Peach Festival, Cobden
Sept.—Harvest Days, Mundelein
Sept.—Heritage Festival, South Holland
Sept.—Harvest Festival, Hanover Park
Sept.—Old-Fashioned Fall Harvest Festival
    Aurora
Sept.—St. Anne Pumpkin Festival, St. Anne
Sept.—Swedish Festival, Glencoe
Sept.—Riverfront Festival, Yorkville
Sept.—Mexican Fiesta Days, Sterling
Sept.—The Great Pumpkin Patch, Lyndon
Sept.—Arnold's Farm Festival, Elizabeth
Sept.—Behmer's Pumpkin Fantasyland,
    Stillman Valley
Sept.—Autumn Pioneer Festival, Belvidere
Sept.—Selmi's Fall Festival, Rock Falls
Sept.—Amish Country Cheese Festival,
    Arthur
Sept.—Ethnic Festival, Springfield
Sept.—Popcorn Festival, Casey
Sept.—Broom Corn Festival, Arcola
Sept.—Apple & Pork Festival, Clinton
Sept.—Grape Festival, Nauvoo
Sept.—Hog Capital of the World Festival,
    Kewanee
Sept.—Warren County Prime Beef Festival,
    Monmouth Park
Sept.—Pumpkin Festival, Morton
Sept.—Agricultural Days Harvest Festival,
    Bishop Hill
Sept.—Apple Festival, Murphysboro
Sept.—Wheat Festival, Okawville
Sept.—Barbecue Championships,
    Murphysboro
Sept.—Annual Applefest, Jerseyville

Index

Index (continued)

Index (continued)

Recipe Contributors

Recipe Contributors (continued)

The Barn of Rockford Bed & Breakfast, Rockford 20

The Eli's Cheesecake Co., Chicago 58

State Journal-Register, Springfield 13, 33

Susie's Garden Patch, Garden Prairie 68

The Village Inn Bed and Breakfast, Arthur 76

Marilyn Lila Thomson, Hillsboro 75

Ellen L. Unger, Charleston 68

Univ. of Illinois, Urbana-Champaign 17

Evelyn VanPuyvelde, Moline 34

Victorian Inn Bed and Breakfast, Rock Island 80

Rebecca Wallace, Collinsville 59

Western Illinois Tourism, Macomb 50

Donna Wilkerson, Dahlgren 14, 16

Susan Williams, Ingleside 47, 84

Florence Wolters, Albers 16

Mrs. Karen Worner, Metamora 37

Diane Zellinske-O'Fallon 73

Jeanette Zinck, Nashville 70

Also Available from Golden West Publishers

HAUNTED HIGHWAY
The Spirits of Route 66

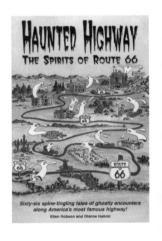

Sixty-six spine-tingling tales of haunted homes, businesses and graveyards along America's "Mother Road." Includes state maps and traveler's information on each site. Read about the ghosts of Chicago's *801 W. Belmont, Red Lion Pub, Biograph Theater* and *Excalibur Club.* Learn about Mary who haunts the *Resurrection Cemetery* in Justice and Midlothian's *Bachelors' Grove Cemetery* where phantom buildings and cars appear. The *Country House* in Clarendon Hills has a pretty ghost as does the *Rialto Square Theater* in Joliet. At Springfield's *Theater Center,* Joe is still waiting for his opening night and the *Dana-Thomas House* and *Abraham Lincoln Home* have resident apparitions. Last but not least, Springfield's *Inn at 835* has a fascinating, playful spirit who oversees daily operations much as she did in the 1800s.

Haunted Highway, The Spirits of Route 66
5 1/2 x 8 1/2 — 192 pages . . . $12.95

ORDER BLANK

GOLDEN WEST PUBLISHERS

☼ 4113 N. Longview Ave. • Phoenix, AZ 85014

www.goldenwestpublishers.com • **1-800-658-5830** • FAX 602-279-6901

Qty	Title	Price	Amount
	Apple Lovers Cook Book	**6.95**	
	Bean Lovers Cook Book	**6.95**	
	Berry Lovers Cook Book	**6.95**	
	Best Barbecue Recipes	**6.95**	
	Chili-Lovers Cook book	**6.95**	
	Corn Lovers Cook Book	**6.95**	
	Easy Recipes for Wild Game & Fish	**6.95**	
	Haunted Highway—The Spirits of Route 66	**12.95**	
	Illinois Cook Book	**6.95**	
	Iowa Cook Book	**6.95**	
	Joy of Muffins	**6.95**	
	Michigan Cook Book	**6.95**	
	Minnesota Cook Book	**6.95**	
	Pumpkin Lovers Cook Book	**6.95**	
	Quick-n-Easy Mexican Recipes	**6.95**	
	Salsa Lovers Cook Book	**6.95**	
	Tequila Cook Book	**7.95**	
	Tortilla Lovers Cook Book	**6.95**	
	Veggie Lovers Cook Book	**6.95**	
	Wisconsin Cook Book	**6.95**	

Shipping & Handling Add: United States $3.00
Canada & Mexico $5.00—All others $12.00

☐ My Check or Money Order Enclosed

☐ MasterCard ☐ VISA ($20 credit card minimum)

Total $ _____

(Payable in U.S. funds)

Acct. No. _____ Exp. Date _____

Signature _____

Name _____ Phone _____

Address _____

City/State/Zip _____

Call for a FREE catalog of all of our titles

4/02   **This order blank may be photocopied**   Illinois Ck Bk